NEW MEXICO

Real Estate Basics

SECOND EDITION

Dearborn™

Real Estate Education

While a great deal of care has been taken to provide accurate and current information, the ideas, suggestions, general principles, and conclusions presented in this text are subject to local, state, and federal laws and regulations, court cases, and any revisions of same. The reader is urged to consult legal counsel regarding any points of law. This publication should not be used as a substitute for competent legal advice.

President: Roy Lipner
Vice-President of Product Development and Publishing: Evan M. Butterfield
Editorial Project Consultant: Marie Spodek, DREI
Development Editor: Elizabeth Austin
Director of Production: Daniel Frey
Typesetting: Janet Schroeder
Creative Director: Lucy Jenkins
Cover and Text Design: Gail Chandler

Contents

Introduction iv
How to Use This Book vi

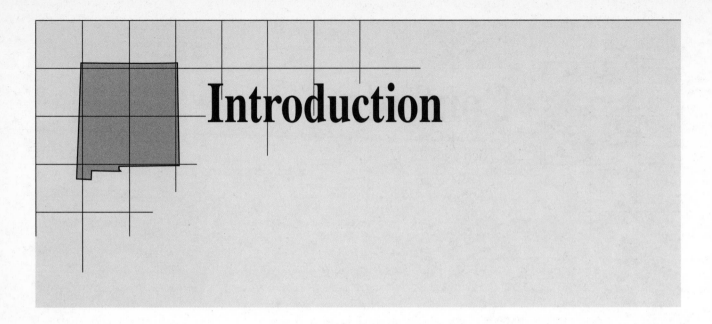

Introduction

Over the last century, all 50 states and the District of Columbia have enacted laws, rules, and regulations to govern the real estate profession. These laws have been enacted to protect the public—buyers, sellers, landlords, and tenants—from dishonest, careless, or unethical practices by real estate licensees. Essentially, the laws provide a framework to ensure that licensees are competent and engage in acceptable business behaviors. Across the United States, some of these laws and regulations are so similar that they can be considered "national" or "generic" real estate principles. Many of the important details, however, vary greatly among the states. To ensure both professional competency and that you pass the licensing exam, it's vital that you understand both the "big picture" principles *and* the state-specific details.

This book has been primarily designed to supplement a general real estate principles text, and you will find a convenient correlation table that illustrates where the general topics are addressed in a variety of other publications. However, *New Mexico Real Estate Basics* also provides a valuable overview of state law and practice when used on its own.

No book writes itself. Like a real estate transaction, this book is the product of teamwork and cooperation among professionals. The following individuals contributed their expertise, industry knowledge, and practical insight to this book.

About the Author

Bill W. McCoy III is a native New Mexican and resides in Albuquerque, New Mexico with his wife of 27 years. They have a daughter and, now, two beautiful granddaughters. Licensed as a New Mexico real estate broker since 1979, he founded New Mexico's largest independent Qualified Intermediary company. Now semiretired, Bill is focusing his efforts in the area of real estate education.

Mr. McCoy is the author of *Introduction to Commercial Real Estate Sales* and a contributing author of *Investment Property Practice and Management,* both published by Dearborn™ Real Estate Education. Bill acts as Dean of Real Estate Education and teaches prelicensing courses for Dearborn Real Estate Institute. Bill also teaches continuing education courses for four universities and numerous professional and government organizations including the New Mexico Society of Public Accountants, the Bureau of Indian Affairs, and eight boards of REALTORS® across New Mexico. In addition, Bill is active with the New Mexico Real Estate Commission and chaired the Education Steering Committee and Rules and Regulations Task Force.

Content Reviewer

Lou Tulga, CCIM, CRB, PhD, Professional Education Services

How to Use This Book

The conversion table below provides a quick and easy reference for *New Mexico Real Estate Basics* in conjunction with various principles books. For instance, *New Mexico Real Estate Basics* Chapter 2, "Operating a Real Estate Business," may be read in conjunction with Chapters 5 and 20 in *Modern Real Estate Practice;* Chapters 7, 9, and 15 in *Real Estate Fundamentals;* Chapters 13, 14, 16, and 17 in *Mastering Real Estate Principles;* and Lessons 13, 14, and 17 in *National Real Estate Principles* software.

New Mexico Real Estate Basics	Modern Real Estate Practice 16th Edition	Real Estate Fundamentals 6th Edition	Mastering Real Estate Principles 4th Edition	National Real Estate Principles Software
1. Licensing Overview	——	——	16	16
2. Operating a Real Estate Business	5, 20	7, 9, 15	13, 14, 16, 17	13, 14, 17
3. Agency Overview	4, 5, 6, 17	9	13, 24	13, 24
4. Contracts and Closings Overview	6, 10, 11, 13, 21, 22	6, 7, 10, 16, 17	3, 10, 11, 12, 14	3, 10, 11, 12, 14
5. License Law Enforcement Overview	4, 5	——	13, 16	13, 16
6. Specialty Topics	8, 16, 18	5, 8, 11	8, 9, 18	8, 9, 18
7. Title Issues	7, 10, 19	3, 10, 14	3, 4, 5	3, 4, 5, 26

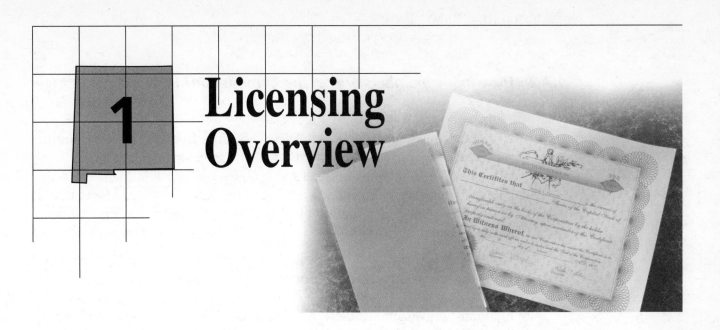

1 Licensing Overview

The New Mexico Statutes Annotated (NMSA), Chapter 61, "Professional Occupational Licenses," govern real estate practices in New Mexico. This law also authorizes the New Mexico Real Estate Commission (NMREC) to adopt a set of administrative rules and regulations to define the statutory law. These are part of the New Mexico Administrative Code, referred to as NMAC throughout this text. The Administrative Rules have the same force and effect as the law and provide more detail for the administration of the law and guidelines for the real estate licensee.

This first chapter covers the licensing agency and licensing issues: activities requiring licensure and exemptions, license categories, and licensing requirements and renewals.

A. New Mexico Real Estate Commission

1.A.1 What is the name of the New Mexico real estate regulatory body?

To regulate real estate activity, New Mexico has a five-member body called the New Mexico Real Estate Commission (NMREC). It is located at 5200 Oakland Avenue NE, Suite B, Albuquerque, New Mexico 87113. Its phone numbers are voice: 505-222-9820, facsimile: 505-222-9886, and toll-free: 800-801-7505. The Web site is *www.state.nm.us/clients/nmrec*.

1.A.2   How many members are on the Commission? How long may they serve?

NMREC is made up of five members who serve five-year terms or until a successor is appointed. The governor makes the appointments. For representational input, four must be licensed brokers and one is a member of the public who has never been licensed. Each must have been a resident of New Mexico for three years, and no more than one Commissioner may be from any one county.

1.A.3   Who does the day-to-day work?

Like most organizations, there are others who help facilitate internal operations. The Commission employs a staff to run the day-to-day functions: licensing, continuing education, and investigation of complaints made against licensees.

The executive secretary plays a crucial role in the administration and implementation of New Mexico's Real Estate Commission policy. The education manager plays a vital role in the implementation of the educational requirements. Neither is a member of the Commission.

1.A.4   NMREC is charged with what statutory duties?

The home Web page of NMREC is *www.state.nm.us/clients/nmrec*. According to this site, the "purpose of the Real Estate Commission is to license real estate brokers, and enforce the New Mexico Real Estate License Law and Commission Rules and Regulations. The Commission meets its regulatory obligation by maintaining a program that protects the public, monitors the Real Estate License Law and Commission Rules and Regulations, and maintains an efficient, inexpensive, and accountable administrative program." The Commission also has jurisdiction over unlicensed individuals who are performing the acts of a broker. License applications and exam dates can be downloaded from this Web site.

The License Law of New Mexico can be changed only by a vote of the legislature, signed by the governor. On the other hand, the Commission may change the rules from time to time after holding formal hearings.

B. Licensing Issues

1.B.1   In New Mexico, who is required to hold a real estate license?

In New Mexico, anyone who does any of the following for others for compensation or consideration must hold a real estate license:

- Lists, sells, or offers to sell real estate
- Buys or offers to buy real estate
- Negotiates the purchase, sale, or exchange of real estate or options on real estate
- Leases, rents, or auctions or offers to lease, rent, or auction real estate

Others who must hold a license include anyone who advertises or represents himself or herself as being engaged as a full-time or part-time real estate broker. Finally, those who are engaged in the business of charging a fee for any publication issued primarily for the purpose of referring information to brokers must also be licensed.

The state takes this authority under the concept of police power, that is, the right of the governing body to enact laws to protect the public. A real estate licensee is in a position to assist or harm the public; hence, the need for licensing.

1.B.2   What is the most important exemption to the licensing requirements?

The most important exemption is the person who acts on his or her own behalf. Any person can list, buy, rent, or sell his or her own property. The state does not regulate such a transaction: if the owner makes a mistake, the owner may hold only himself or herself responsible, no one else.

1.B.3   Are there any other exemptions to the licensing requirements?

By extension, *anyone who is employed by the owner of the property (on a regular full-time basis)* is exempt from licensure requirements in order to buy, sell, or manage property owned, rented, leased, or to be acquired by this owner (except in the case of a subdivision of more than 99 lots). Others who are exempt include the following: lawyers when acting as such, government employees and court-appointed individuals, trustees, brokers of severed mineral interests, and persons operating under power of attorney for final consummation of a transaction (limited to twice a year unless related by fourth degree of consanguinity).

1.B.4 Does New Mexico recognize licensure in other states?

New Mexico may enter into specific licensure recognition agreements on a state-by-state basis. The Commission may enter into agreements for full recognition if the other state has substantially similar initial licensing requirements. As of April 2005, the New Mexico Real Estate Commission has license recognition agreements in place with Colorado, Georgia, Oklahoma, Utah, and Montana.

The licensee must complete an application form and sign an irrevocable consent that any lawsuits and actions may be brought against them in the proper court of any New Mexico county in which a cause of action may arise. Simply stated, if a legal action is initiated, the licensee cannot request a change of venue.

If the home-state license of a nonresident New Mexico licensee is revoked or suspended, the licensee must notify NMREC. A hearing may be held to determine whether similar disciplinary action should be taken against the licensee in New Mexico.

1.B.5 May a corporation or partnership receive a real estate license?

Yes. On compliance with the act, a member, employee, or officer of the corporation or partnership must obtain a license. The license will allow the entity and the licensed member to conduct real estate brokerage.

1.B.6 What is the difference between a qualifying broker and an associate broker? Can there be more than one broker in any given office?

The practices of the real estate industry are similar to the old master craftsman–apprentice system of years ago. Real estate licensees with an associate broker's license must work under the direct supervision of a qualifying broker. All licensees associated with a qualifying broker must have a written employment or independent contractor agreement. All licenses must be prominently displayed in the broker's office.

New Mexico has single licensure, so all licensees are classified as either qualifying brokers or associate brokers. Persons holding salesperson's licenses on January 1, 2006 were grandfathered in as associate brokers with no further requirements.

Each real estate office must be under the direct control and supervision of a qualifying broker. When the license law refers to a qualifying broker, it is referring to this individual. The other people in the office may hold associate brokers' licenses. The qualifying broker may be the owner or a manager. The qualifying broker is responsible for all trust accounts and for the real estate activities conducted by the associates in this office.

The public has the right to know who is responsible for the office activities. The Commission requires signage with two-inch letters clearly identifying the firm and the qualifying broker. Even if the office is owned by another entity in another city, the qualifying broker is responsible for the trust monies held by that office and the activities of each person licensed in that office. All brokerage contracts are in the name of the broker.

1.B.7   List the basic requirements for a real estate license.

An applicant for a New Mexico real estate license must be at least 18 years of age, a legal resident of the United States, and of good repute. The applicant must pass the test after meeting the minimum education requirements and be competent to transact business in such a way as to safeguard the public. To ensure good repute, the applicant must include recommendations from two reputable citizens who own real estate in the county they reside or work in.

1.B.8   What are some reasons the Commission may deny a license?

Any decision made to deny a license must follow the Uniform Licensing Act (ULA). Thus, any action to deny, suspend, or revoke requires a hearing, and the results of the hearing can be appealed to District Court pursuant to the ULA. The Commission must follow the Criminal Offenders Employment Act.

The Commission may refuse, suspend, or revoke a license for any of the reasons listed in 61-29-12 NMSA 1978. Reasons include misrepresentations, paying unlicensed individuals, failing to properly handle trust monies, conviction of a felony or crime involving moral turpitude, discipline in another license jurisdiction, or any act constituting bad faith, dishonesty, incompetency, impropriety, fraud, negligence, or other unlawful act. Under the Parental Responsibility Act, an applicant can be denied a license, and a licensee can be denied renewal for failure to pay child support.

Fees remitted with an application for licensure are refunded if the Commission finds the applicant was not qualified for a license.

1.B.9   Will the Commission make any exceptions?

Possibly, yes. If denied a license, the ULA requires a hearing, and the applicant has 20 days to request a hearing. The Commission will consider the nature of an offense, any documented aggravating or extenuating circumstances, time lapsed, rehabilitation, treatment, and restitution performed before denying or revoking a license.

1.B.10   Are any special duties imposed on qualifying brokers?

The qualifying broker must maintain, if a resident broker, a place of business within New Mexico. The broker must prominently display his or her own license and the licenses of all other licensees affiliated with that qualifying broker in the office at the address as registered with the Commission. Although the license law, rules, and regulations are available on the Internet, each broker must have in the place of business and available to all licensees a current hard copy of the *State of New Mexico Real Estate License Law and Rules and Regulations Manual.*

The qualifying broker must supervise all real estate-related activities conducted on behalf of others by the associated licensees and maintain current written employment or independent contractor agreements with them. The broker is responsible for paying commissions. The broker must also maintain full and complete records of all real estate-related matters processed through the brokerage. A qualifying broker who is going to be absent for a time exceeding seven days must designate a broker-in-charge and inform the Commission in writing of the designation. The broker-in-charge then assumes the responsibilities of the qualifying broker.

The required records must be available to the Commission or any duly authorized representative at the place of business of the qualifying broker or at the Real Estate Commission office. All such records shall be retained for a period of not less than three years. The broker is responsible for depositing all money received on behalf of others in the proper trust account as soon after receipt as practicably possible after securing signatures of all parties to the transaction.

1.B.11   Do the affiliated licensees have any responsibilities?

The affiliated licensees may not engage in any real estate activities for others for which a real estate license is required outside the knowledge and supervision of their qualifying broker or broker-in-charge. They may not receive any commissions or fees related to real estate activities for which a license is required from anyone other than their qualifying broker or broker-in-charge.

Affiliate licensees may conduct all real estate-related business for others only in the trade name of the brokerage as registered with the Commission. They must remit all monies of others, including checks and promissory notes, related to transactions to the qualifying broker or broker-in-charge as soon after receipt as practicably possible after securing signatures of all parties to the transaction. Finally, they must maintain all transaction files in the office of the brokerage.

1.B.12 Can an associate broker be licensed under more than one broker?

No, associate brokers cannot be licensed under more than one broker during the same time period. Moreover, in the situation of a licensee who hires a licensed personal assistant, both must be licensed under the same broker. While it is possible for an individual to become a qualifying broker for more than one entity (corporation or partnership), it is not possible to have more than one license in an individual capacity.

1.B.13 What are the specific requirements for an applicant to obtain an associate broker's license?

Qualified applicants for licensure as an associate broker must successfully complete 90 hours of Commission-approved courses, including a 30-hour broker basics course. The completion certificate is valid for 36 months.

In other words, after course completion, the candidate has three years to take and pass the state-required real estate examination. Evidence of compliance is required at the testing site to prove that the required prelicensing course work was completed.

1.B.14 What are the additional requirements to become a qualifying broker?

There are several different ways to qualify for a broker's license in New Mexico. The first is to be actively licensed as an associate broker for at least 24 of the preceding 36 months and to complete 120 hours of classroom instruction in approved real estate courses. The specific classes include 30 hours in real estate law, 30 hours in real estate practice, and 30 hours in broker basics.

Finally, an out-of-state broker may provide documented current licensure as a real estate broker in another state for at least two years. This candidate must have completed 120 hours of classroom instruction in approved real estate courses. A current license history from the other state's licensing agency is required.

1.B.15 Who administers the real estate exam?

The computerized examination is designed to establish the competency of the applicant to protect the interests of the public. A Commission-contracted provider conducts the real estate examination. This provider offers computerized testing through a network of testing centers. The test is made up of 130 items: 40 relating to New Mexico laws, rules, and regulations and 90 pertinent to general real estate principles and practices. Each portion contains five unscored items. Candidates must score at least 75 percent on each portion within four hours.

1.B.16 Who pays for the exam?

The candidate pays the examination fee directly to the Real Estate Commission. The Commission establishes the examination fees.

1.B.17 May a candidate who fails the exam retake it?

A person who fails to pass ei ther portion of the real estate exam is allowed to immediately retake the failed portion of the exam by telephoning or filing a new registration form with the testing service and paying the examination fee. There is no limit to the number of times that the applicant may take the exam.

The retake fee is $95 for either or both parts of the exam, and all candidates must pass both parts of the exam within 90 days.

1.B.18 What is the next step after the person passes the exam?

On successful completion of the exam, the applicant receives at the test site a passing notice and a Commission-approved application. Candidates who pass the exam must file for a license with the Commission within 60 days; otherwise, the passing test results are nullified and the exam must be retaken. However, an extension may be granted because of military service or extenuating circumstances.

In addition to the completed application form, the application package to NMREC must include the following:

- Qualifying broker-signed application
- Sealed credit report
- The passing notice
- Proof of the required education
- Compliance with mandatory errors and omissions insurance
- Recommendations from two reputable citizens
- Appropriate licensure fee

Also, because a credit report is required, candidates should submit documentation regarding any credit discrepancies such as tax liens, judgments, foreclosures, past-due child support, and past-due amounts. Otherwise, the application may be delayed for several weeks.

2005 law changes have authorized the Commission to require criminal background checks for all license applicants.

1.B.19 How are license fees determined?

Maximum fees are set by statute. The Commission sets the actual fees for licensing based on the administrative costs of sustaining the Commission.

As of January 2004, the license fee charged for a three-year license is $240.

1.B.20 Can the first-time applicant ask for an inactive license?

Yes; initial applicants are allowed to file for an "inactive" license. Individuals whose licenses are on inactive status with NMREC are not required to carry errors and omissions insurance. However, they are still required to complete the same amount of continuing education as an active licensee.

1.B.21   When does a real estate license expire?

All licenses are issued for three-year terms, expiring on the last day of the month following the licensee's month of birth. For example, if the licensee's birthday is September 7, the license will expire on October 31.

1.B.22   Does the Commission require a credit check?

Yes; as previously noted, applicants must submit a sealed credit report along with their applications. If there are any credit discrepancies, such as tax liens, judgments, foreclosures, past-due child support, and past-due amounts, the applicant should supply explanations.

1.B.23   Are there any residency or citizenship requirements?

In New Mexico, applicants must be legal residents of the United States.

1.B.24   How is a license renewed?

Renewal applications are mailed to each licensee whose license is due for renewal. However, failure to receive the renewal notice does not relieve the licensee of this duty to renew. The licensee must submit the application form and pay the appropriate renewal fee. Renewal fees are the same as the ones for original licensure, $240.

1.B.25   How many continuing education hours are required for active status renewal?

The licensee must complete a minimum of 30 approved continuing education hours. Each licensee must complete the eight-hour Commission-approved mandatory course plus 22 hours of Commission-approved elective course work. These hours cannot be carried over to another license term. The applicant must submit certificates from each course. Licensees over age 65 with 20 years' consecutive licensing are exempt from continuing education requirements.

1.B.26   Is there any alternative to attending continuing education classes for renewal purposes?

The Commission recognizes computer-based training and correspondence courses for all but the mandatory eight hours. Up to four hours of credit are given for attending a Commission meeting, rules hearing, or disciplinary hearing.

1.B.27   What are the consequences if the license is not timely renewed?

If the licensee fails to renew by the appropriate expiration date, the license expires. The person is given the opportunity to renew by paying three times the normal renewal fee for up to one year after expiration. However, once the license expires, no real estate business can be conducted until a new "active" license is issued. In other words, the grace period is to renew, but not to act.

1.B.28   Are there any provisions to renew a license after the grace period?

No, there are none. The licensee may be required take the required education hours and repass the exam.

C. Licensee Duties and Responsibilities

1.C.1   Who keeps track of each license?

Each affiliate's license must be displayed in the qualifying broker's office. Each licensee is responsible for maintaining active licensure and for fulfilling renewal duties.

1.C.2   Is it legal for a licensee to buy and/or sell property for his or her own portfolio?

Licensees are not allowed to act as undisclosed principals in any transaction. Without disclosure, there is a conflict of interest and an appearance of impropriety. Written disclosure is required when licensees act on behalf of their immediate families.

Before buying, selling, or leasing real estate in New Mexico, licensees must give written disclosure to all parties of any ownership or interest that they have or will have in the transaction. All licensees (including inactive licensees) who list their property must include on the listing the fact that the owner is licensed. On the purchase agreement, the licensee must include a remark that *the purchaser is licensed.*

The rules require that any *conflict of interest* created be discussed with both the seller-client and the buyer-client at the time of or prior to the licensee's solicitation of confidential information, prior to an offer being made by the buyer, or prior to an acceptance by the seller. Thus, a licensee is allowed to purchase property from seller-clients or sell property owned by the licensee to buyer-clients *only if* the licensee includes a clearly written disclosure describing his or her true position to the other party.

1.C.3 May licensees sell or buy property for themselves without going through their brokers?

The statutes do not address this issue. Most brokers cover it in the employment contract.

1.C.4 Under what conditions may a real estate licensee hire a support person (unlicensed assistant)?

Many top producers hire a support person(s) to assist them. These assistants may be licensed or not licensed.

1.C.5 Who is legally responsible for the activities performed by the unlicensed assistant?

In New Mexico, affiliated licensees who engage unlicensed assistants are referred to as Responsible Persons in the rules, and have the primary responsibility for their supervision. Obviously, firms or qualifying brokers have supervisory responsibilities for the acts or activities of licensed personal assistants, but the primary responsibility rests with the persons who employed them.

1.C.6 What are some of the activities that an unlicensed person may perform?

A complete list of activities that an unlicensed person may perform can be found in the commission rules (New Mexico Administrative Code) 16 NMAC 61.21.8. Essentially, unlicensed persons may perform secretarial activities and maintenance activities, but may not represent themselves as being licensees or perform any acts with consumers that require a real estate license.

Briefly, under the direct supervision of a licensee, New Mexico law permits unlicensed assistants to answer the telephone and provide listing information to other licensees as well as to forward calls from the public to a licensee. An unlicensed assistant can schedule an open house, perform physical maintenance, and accompany a licensee to an open house or a showing and function as a host. At the open house, the unlicensed assistant may not discuss, negotiate, or solicit offers for the property or provide any information other than printed material prepared and approved by the licensee (i.e., responsible person). All inquiries must be referred to the licensee (responsible person).

In addition, the unlicensed assistant is allowed to receive, record, and deposit earnest money, security deposits, and advance rents, although the qualifying broker and responsible person are still responsible for all actions.

Unlicensed assistants may also perform the following duties:

- Submit listing data to the multiple-listing service
- Check on the status of closing files
- Assemble documents for closing
- Have keys made
- Write advertisements (provided that the ads are approved by the qualifying broker)
- Place signs on property
- Act as a courier
- Schedule appointments to show the property with the seller or seller's agent
- Arrange dates and times for inspections, mortgage applications, walk-through inspections, and closings
- Provide to the public preprinted property information that has been prepared by a licensee

1.C.7   What activities are specifically prohibited for an unlicensed assistant?

A complete list of prohibited activities may be found in 16 NMAC 61.21.9. New Mexico laws prohibit unlicensed assistants from using the telephone or acting in person to prospect for listings, leases, buyers, Section 1031 tax-deferred exchange candidates, or property management contracts.

In addition, they are prohibited from hosting open houses, kiosks, home-show booths, or fairs independent of their licensed employer.

Showing property without the licensed employer being present is strictly prohibited. Answering any real estate-related question germane to the actual transaction is prohibited.

One final note, just to clarify: unlicensed personal assistants are not allowed to represent themselves in any manner as being licensed or affiliated with a particular firm for conducting real estate business.

1.C.8   Are there any exceptions to the foregoing?

Yes; if the licensee is a qualified person with a disability, as defined in the Americans with Disabilities Act, the unlicensed assistant may provide assistance that constitutes reasonable accommodation to the licensee. However, the licensee must be in direct control of the activities and as close as practical to the activity. The assistant may not even appear to have the authority to act as a licensee. The licensee must notify the Commission of the identity of all unlicensed assistants who perform for the licensee services normally requiring a license pursuant to this rule before performance of these services.

2 Operating a Real Estate Business

With a qualifying broker's license, one may open and operate a real estate business. The qualifying broker may hire those holding an associate broker's license, although the qualifying broker is ultimately responsible for the actions of affiliated licensees. This chapter covers the additional rules and regulations for brokers regarding advertising and trust accounts. Additionally, real estate licensees must comply with state variations to federal laws. These variations to federal fair housing laws and Megan's Law are noted.

A. Office Licenses

2.A.1 What licenses are required before a qualifying broker can open an office?

A person planning to open a real estate office must hold a qualifying broker's license and the appropriate local business license.

2.A.2 How does a corporation or partnership receive a real estate license?

A partnership, association, or corporation is not granted a license unless every member and/or employee who actively participates in the brokerage business holds a real estate license. At least one member, called the qualifying broker, has to hold a broker's license.

2.A.3 How many licenses must a branch office have?

Each office must have a qualifying broker license, with the exception of a temporary field office. The Real Estate Commission has final authority to determine if an office is either a temporary or a branch office. Running a temporary office is the only situation in which an associate broker may run an office. The associate broker must still be under the supervision of a qualifying broker in the main office.

2.A.4 Under what circumstances may a qualifying broker open a temporary office?

Temporary or field offices are often used when marketing a subdivision of lots or new homes. The qualifying broker may have full-time staff at the location, but does not establish an office for licensing purposes.

B. Advertising Rules

2.B.1 What is a blind ad? Is it legal in New Mexico?

In New Mexico, a **blind ad** is one in which a brokerage firm or listing agent includes just his or her own name, a post office box number, or a telephone number to bait readers into believing that the advertised property is being offered for sale by a private party. This unscrupulous practice is illegal.

All licensees, when advertising real estate for others, must use their regular business name and telephone number as registered with the Commission. Real estate advertising must be honest. It should never be misleading or deceptive or intentionally misrepresent any property, terms, values, or policies and services of the brokerage. The qualifying broker must supervise and is responsible for all advertising.

2.B.2 Are there special requirements for a real estate office to advertise on the Internet?

There are no specific requirements for Internet advertising. They are the same for all media. All licensees, when advertising property for others, must use the office trade name and telephone number as registered with the Commission.

2.B.3   Under what circumstances may a brokerage place a For Sale sign?

A broker may place a For Sale sign on a property with written permission of the owner. Failure to remove a sign when requested violates New Mexico Commission rules and is subject to disciplinary action. After a sold listing closes, the new owner must consent to leave a sold sign up.

C. Trust Accounts

2.C.1   What is trust money, and what can a qualifying broker do with it?

Trust money is money of others related to a specific transaction or property management account. Every New Mexico real estate brokerage firm that expects to handle funds belonging to others must place that money in an authorized trust account, identified by the words *trust account,* in a bank, savings association, or title company authorized to do business in New Mexico. The qualifying broker is responsible for all trust account records and duplicate transaction files.

2.C.2   Where can trust funds be located?

The account must be styled as the trust account of the broker. The trust account and trade name must appear on all account documents. Trust account funds must be deposited in a bank, savings association, or title company authorized to do business in New Mexico. In a multi-office company, trust account records may be maintained and retained at the main/corporate office provided the qualifying broker notifies the Commission in writing.

All such records and funds are subject to inspection by the Commission or its authorized representative at the designated New Mexico office location or at the Commission offices. The records must include, as a minimum, clear indication of all funds received and disbursed on behalf of others in all real estate transactions when the qualifying broker is involved. All records must be under the direct control and supervision of the qualifying broker.

2.C.3   How soon must trust funds be deposited?

All funds belonging to others, unless agreed to between contracting parties, must be deposited into the broker's trust account *as soon as practicably possible after the last signature of acceptance.* This signed, dated instrument could be an offer to purchase, a rental agreement, a lease, an exchange, or even an option. However, prior to obtaining *the last signature,* it is customary to keep earnest money checks in the transaction file of the listing broker.

2.C.4   How is the earnest money handled when one office has the listing and another office is working with the buyer?

In the case of a cooperative sale, the listing broker may elect to have the buyer make the earnest money check payable to the listing firm's trust account. If a cooperative buyer's broker receives cash, the buyer's agent can deposit the cash into the buyer broker's trust account and then issue a check to the listing company's trust account. The licensee is responsible for maintaining a paper trail to properly account for the cash received.

2.C.5   What if a buyer wants to use a postdated check or a diamond ring for earnest money?

In New Mexico, the Commission rules do not address postdated checks or anything other than cash or an immediately cashable check. Licensees should be careful to clearly communicate any of these situations to the seller prior to acceptance of the offer and to ascertain that the nature of the "deposit" as well as any obligations of the broker in handling the item is clearly stated in the offer to purchase.

2.C.6   What are the rules governing a trust account?

Unless there is a written agreement between all parties to the contrary, trust accounts in New Mexico may not earn interest. The rules do allow for establishment of special or custodial trust accounts by written agreement, and these may be interest-bearing accounts. Trust funds to be placed in a custodial account first must be placed in a regular trust account and then transferred to the custodial account.

The qualifying broker must keep detailed records of all funds received. The qualifying broker is responsible for indicating the date received and deposited, from whom received, and for which property transaction. Finally, the broker must clearly indicate the nature of the funds, that is, earnest money deposit, rents, security deposit, owners' funds, and so forth.

Likewise, the qualifying broker must maintain a detailed record of all funds disbursed. Records maintained by the broker must clearly indicate the following: check number, date of payment, payee, amount and purpose of payment, and the related property transaction.

A check numbering system with a check register must be used for control purposes, and voided checks must be retained. Trust account bank records and office records must be reconciled monthly. The broker must keep these records for at least three years.

2.C.7   How can a qualifying broker open a trust account without any trust funds?

The state of New Mexico allows the qualifying broker to open trust accounts using personal funds not to exceed the required minimum balance in order to meet the minimum balance requirements of the bank necessary to maintain the account and avoid charges. Such use of these funds is not considered commingling.

2.C.8   What is commingling of funds and why is it illegal?

By definition, **commingling** is mixing personal funds with those belonging to other people. To repeat, the qualifying broker's personal funds are to be used solely for paying expenses directly related to the maintenance of the trust account.

The problem with excess personal funds in the broker's trust account is simple. If the qualifying broker commingled personal funds into this account and the IRS froze the broker's accounts, then the trust account would be frozen, too. The same thing could happen if a sole proprietor owned the brokerage and suddenly died after commingling personal funds into the trust account. The commingled brokerage trust account could end up in probate. In either event, all closings would be tied up for a considerable length of time.

To avoid these potential problems, brokers may not keep more personal funds in this account than the balance required by the institution. Also included in the definition of commingling are funds that the qualifying broker is entitled to but that have not been withdrawn within a reasonable time.

The statutes list other examples of illegally commingled funds. Examples include allowing a rental property owner's fund within a trust account to become deficient and placing monies from the management of the qualifying broker's own properties in a trust account containing funds of others. On the other hand, if a written agreement exists between the qualifying broker and the property owner, funds from two or more properties owned by that property owner may be commingled in the same fund.

2.C.9   What happens to unclaimed trust funds?

The qualifying broker may disburse trust account overages only in accordance with the Unclaimed Property Act and after written notification to the Commission.

2.C.10   What may not be paid directly out of the trust account?

It should be noted that the qualifying broker should never use the trust account as his or her business operating account or for personal needs. Monies that may not be disbursed directly from this account include salaries and normal business or operational expenses. The qualifying broker can pay company commissions or commissions to other companies only from the operating or business account.

The qualifying broker or designee may not disburse trust funds for the personal use of the broker. Commissions may be paid only to the qualifying broker, and commission splits may not be paid directly from any trust account. The qualifying broker must obtain the written consent and signatures of all parties to the transaction before disbursing funds from the trust account. However, the broker may transfer trust funds to another Commission-approved trust account or title company. Finally, the broker is not allowed to disburse funds in excess of the actual amount in the account.

2.C.11   What is the procedure for disbursing trust funds?

As a general rule, no funds can be disbursed from the trust account prior to the closing without the informed written consent of all the parties.

In the event of a dispute over the return or forfeiture of any earnest money or escrow deposit held by the broker, the qualifying broker is required to hold the deposit in the trust account until he or she receives written consent from both parties or a court order directing disbursement.

2.C.12   What is an example of money in and out of a trust account?

It is possible for a qualifying broker to place an earnest money deposit into the trust account and at closing, with written permission, transfer the earnest money to the brokerage account in lieu of commission earned. For example, a broker listed a lot at a price that would yield a $1,000 commission. It sold for full price, and a $1,000 earnest money check was written and deposited into the qualifying broker's trust account.

At closing, the owner of the property gave the qualifying broker written permission to keep the $1,000 earnest money (located in the trust account) in lieu of the commission owed. The $1,000 earnest money held in the trust account, due and payable now as commission earned, must be promptly withdrawn and transferred to the broker's business account or the qualifying broker could be found guilty of unlawful commingling.

2.C.13   What procedures must the qualifying broker follow when the buyer and seller disagree as to how the earnest money should be distributed?

Under certain conditions, the qualifying broker is authorized to release disputed earnest money without written consent of the parties. One example is when the qualifying broker is in receipt of a final judgment of the court directing the disposition of the deposit or there is a final decision of a binding alternative dispute resolution. Another example is when a civil action is filed to determine the disposition of the earnest money, at which time the qualifying broker may seek court authorization to pay the deposit into the court (an interpleader action).

2.C.14   How soon do buyers get their earnest money back when they withdraw their offer before it was accepted?

Obviously, a written release is not required when a seller rejects an offer or buyers withdraw their offer before notification of acceptance. In both events, the earnest money is returned to the buyer without delay. In New Mexico, it is customary for licensees to keep earnest money checks in their transaction files until offer acceptance. If the offer does not result in a contract, the earnest money check is simply returned to the buyer or tenant.

2.C.15   Can the qualifying broker take his or her commission directly from the earnest money in the trust account if the buyer and seller agree, just before closing, to rescind the contract?

No, the qualifying broker may not take his or her fees directly from the trust account. Should a transaction fail to consummate, the broker under no circumstances is entitled to withhold any portion of the earnest money, even though a commission is earned.

For example, sellers accepted an offer for the sale of their home accompanied by a $2,000 earnest money check. After acceptance, the buyers asked the sellers to let them out of the contract due to an unexpected job transfer. The owners agreed and told the buyers they could have their earnest money back, too. In this case, when the sellers accepted the buyers' offer, a commission was earned; however, the listing broker cannot hold the buyers' earnest money hostage. The qualifying broker must return the earnest money as directed and look to the seller for compensation for services rendered.

2.C.16   Is there any other information about keeping proper records of the trust account?

Qualifying brokers may elect to place their trust accounts at an institution that participates in the Land Title Trust Fund Act. In this situation, interest earned on the account is paid to the trust fund administered by the New Mexico Mortgage Finance Authority to fund "first-time buyer" loans in New Mexico.

2.C.17 May property management funds, that is, security deposits, be handled differently?

When managing more than five rental units, the qualifying broker must establish a separate property management trust account. Separate records must be maintained for each property. Deficit accounting and commingling funds from different properties are prohibited.

There is an exception to commingling funds from two or more properties. The owner of multiple properties may give written authorization to commingle funds from the multiple properties.

2.C.18 Any special rules regarding tenants' security deposits?

If the tenant gives written consent, tenant deposits may be turned over to the owner of the property. The landlord or his manager must return to the tenant all security deposits and account for deductions within 30 days of lease termination. The manager must send a statement to the owner monthly (or as agreed), and within 45 days of termination, the manager must provide final accounting. Security deposits are also addressed in the New Mexico Owner Resident Relations Act.

D. Antidiscrimination in New Mexico

2.D.1 What state agency is responsible for enforcing New Mexico's fair housing laws?

The state agency that handles fair housing complaints is the Human Rights Commission of the Human Rights Division of the New Mexico Department of Labor. The Human Rights Division is responsible for enforcing the New Mexico Human Rights Act of 1969 and state executive orders affecting human rights. The division also offers educational programs to employees and employers on unlawful discrimination to prevent discrimination in the workplace.

For more information, contact the Human Rights Commission at 505-827-6838 or 800-566-9471. The Web site is *www.dol.state.nm.us/dol_hrd.html.*

2.D.2   Is the New Mexico fair housing law similar to the federal fair housing laws?

The New Mexico Human Rights Act applies to all types of real estate transactions, not just housing. The exemptions are the same as in the federal act. However, New Mexico has added additional protected classes to those in the federal law. In addition to race, color, religion, national origin, sex, and handicap, New Mexico has added spousal affiliation, sexual orientation, gender identity, and ancestry. The complainant has 180 days to file a complaint.

2.D.3   How is a complaint dealt with?

First, the division accepts the complaint and invites the parties to mediate the case through the Alternative Dispute Resolution (ADR) program. If mediation is not possible, the division investigates to see if there is a prima facie case of discrimination. The investigation is completed and a determination is issued.

If the division does not find probable cause for discrimination, the case is dismissed, although it may be appealed to the District Court. If there is a probable cause, a hearing is set before the Human Rights Commission. After hearing testimony, the commission may issue a written ruling. If the commission finds for the complainant, the commission may award actual damages, compensatory damages, and attorneys' fees.

E. Megan's Law in New Mexico

2.E.1   Are real estate licensees under any obligations regarding Megan's Law?

Briefly, Megan's Law requires that certain sex offenders, when released from prison, must register where they live with the local police. The state is required to maintain a registry of the information and make it available to the public.

The New Mexico information is available through the local law enforcement agencies or at *www.nmsexoffender.com*. New Mexico's version does not address a real estate licensee's duty to discover or to disclose any information about the location of sex offenders. The New Mexico Real Estate Commission Rules state that *data* from the sex offender registry is not considered an adverse material fact.

3 Agency Overview

B rokerage involves bringing together two consumers, buyer and seller or landlord and tenant, to enter into a contract to sell, buy, rent, or manage real property in exchange for a fee. The state regulates the actions by the qualifying broker and his or her affiliated licensees who work with the consumer. Depending on the circumstance, the brokerage may work *for* a consumer-client or work *with* a consumer-customer.

Because consumers rely on real estate licensees for information, it is imperative that they understand the type of representation, if any, they can expect from a licensee. This chapter deals with brokerage relationships, agency concepts, agency disclosures, brokerage agreements, and antitrust laws.

A. Brokerage Relationship Issues

3.A.1 What are brokerage relationships?

Brokerage relationships are the legal or contractual relationships between licensees and consumers when working together in a regulated real estate transaction. The New Mexico legislature and Commission rules have established the relationship between licensees and consumers as transaction broker, unless the parties agree specifically in writing to the creation of a fiduciary (agency) relationship. Consumers may work with licensees as transaction brokers, exclusive agents, or dual agents.

3.A.2 What is a transaction broker?

Transaction broker is the default relationship between licensees and consumers, unless the parties enter into an express written agreement creating an agency relationship. Licensees acting as transaction brokers owe consumers basic duties, as outlined in the Commission Rules and Regulations.

3.A.3 Is a written agreement required before working with a consumer?

A licensee may choose to work with or without a written agreement. However, a written agreement is required for an agency relationship. Also, licensees must remember that New Mexico statutes require a written agreement before a licensee may go to court to collect a commission or fee.

3.A.4 What duties does the licensee owe the consumer in a transaction broker relationship?

The licensee owes the consumer of real estate-related services who is not being represented by the licensee certain duties that do not rise to the status of fiduciary duties. These basic duties include disclosure of any adverse material fact actually known by the licensee about the property or the transaction. However, the licensee is not required to disclose data from a sex offender registry or the existence of group homes.

The licensee must disclose any adverse facts pertaining to the financial ability of the parties to complete the transaction and must promptly account for all monies and property received. As previously mentioned (see 1.C.2 and 1.C.3), the licensee must disclose any material interest or relationship of a business, personal, or family nature. The licensee must keep confidential any information learned in the course of any prior agency relationship, unless the former client specifically consents to disclosure or the law requires disclosure.

The licensee must present all offers in a timely manner and perform any oral or written agreements made with the parties. The licensee must assist all parties according to local, state, and federal fair housing and antidiscrimination laws and help them comply with the terms and conditions of the contract and with the closing of the transaction. Finally, the licensee should suggest that the consumer obtain expert advice concerning matters beyond the scope of the licensee's expertise.

3.A.5 How is agency defined in New Mexico?

In real estate transactions, **agency** means a fiduciary relationship in which a real estate licensee acts for or represents another as an agent, created *only* by the other person's *express written authority* in a transaction. The relationship is built on mutual respect, trust, honesty, and promise keeping.

One party, called the *client, delegates authority* to his or her agent who, in return, *consents* to act for that client. In addition to the basic duties owed to all consumers, the agent will owe the principal (client) fiduciary duties of obedience, loyalty, disclosure, confidentiality, accounting, and reasonable care, as defined by the Real Estate Commission.

3.A.6   By what authority does the agent act?

In the case of a seller-client, the seller could elect to sell his or her home without the services of an agent but, instead, elects to *delegate* the task to an agent. The agent receives (from the seller) *express written authority* to procure a buyer, and by *written authority* receives permission to put up a sign, use a lockbox system (in the owner's absence) to gain entry into the home, and be present during offer negotiations. However, the agent does not have authority to bind the seller to an offer.

3.A.7   What is a special agency?

When the agent is hired to perform a specific task or transaction, a **special agency** is created. In the preceding scenario, the listing agent's authority is very limited. The listing agent is a special agent; that is, one who is hired for a short term and receives limited authority. Agency agreements spell out the agency relationship.

Even if all of the terms of the listing agreement are met, the seller's agent does not have legal authority to bind the seller to an offer, no matter how excellent. Even though a commission may have been earned, the seller's agent has no authority to bind the seller to the offer.

3.A.8   What is a general agency?

A **general agency** is created when the agent is empowered to represent the principal in a broad range of matters related to a particular business or activity. The general agent may, for example, bind the principal to any contract within the scope of the agent's authority.

A property manager is typically a general agent for the owner. Likewise, a licensee affiliated with the qualifying broker is a general agent. The key terms are *long-term* and *broad authority*.

3.A.9   What is single (exclusive) agency?

In single agency, the agent represents only one party in a single transaction in a fiduciary capacity. The agent owes fiduciary duties exclusively to one principal, who may be either a seller/landlord or a buyer/tenant. Any third party is a customer. A customer is a consumer who is not being represented by a licensee but for whom the licensee may perform real estate services.

A seller's agent is an agent who singularly *represents the seller* in a real estate transaction, sometimes referred to as the *listing agent.* The buyer is then considered the customer. A buyer's agent is an agent who singularly *represents the buyer* in a real estate transaction and is often referred to simply as the *buyer's agent.* In buyer agency, the seller is the customer of the buyer's agent.

Many real estate transactions in New Mexico are single agency. The listing company represents the seller, and the cooperating broker represents the buyer. In some offices, the qualifying broker may choose **designated agency.** Under designated agency, one licensee is appointed to exclusively represent the seller; another licensee in the same office is appointed to exclusively represent the buyer.

3.A.10   *What is dual agency, and is it legal in New Mexico?*

New Mexico law authorizes the use of *disclosed dual agency,* provided the brokerage has a company policy permitting its use. **Dual agency** is created when both parties to a transaction give *written authority* to one licensee to represent both parties as an agent in the transaction. Dual agency also occurs when the qualifying broker of the firm is an agent for either party and an affiliated licensee is agent for the other. An individual using dual agency is really not representing either party to the transaction. Instead he or she becomes a facilitator, not taking sides in the negotiation.

In offices that do not choose designated agency, dual agency may also occur when two affiliated licensees represent parties in the same transaction. The practice of dual agency requires *informed, written authority* in the form of a separate dual agency agreement.

3.A.11   *What is designated agency?*

In New Mexico, the qualifying broker may *designate* different licensees affiliated with the brokerage, to exclusively represent clients in an in-house transaction. These **designated agents** work as exclusive agents for either the seller or buyer, *to the exclusion* of all the other licensees within the brokerage. Therefore, two licensees (from the same real estate brokerage) end up representing opposite sides in a single real estate transaction without creating a dual agency.

Under New Mexico rules, a designated agent is not considered a dual agent. Remember, dual agency cannot exist unless the agent personally represents both the buyer and the seller or the licensee's qualifying broker also represents one of the parties as an agent. Using designated agents is an effort to avoid the potential conflict of interests inherent in dual agency and to clarify that not every licensee within a brokerage represents every client of the brokerage.

3.A.12   Who is a customer and what does the agent owe the customer?

A **customer** is a consumer of real estate-related services who has no written agreement with the licensee. While providing brokerage services to customers, licensees must do so *honestly* and in *good faith*. They must diligently exercise reasonable skill and care, and licensees must disclose all adverse material facts that they know. In addition, there is a duty to account for any customer's property that comes into a licensee's possession.

3.A.13   Who is the licensee's client and what does the licensee owe this client?

A client is a party to a transaction who has a written agreement with a licensee for brokerage services. Another name for a client is *the principal*. The principal is the individual who hires and delegates authority to a broker to represent his or her interests. The principal can be the seller, landlord, buyer, or tenant. The broker may represent the principal as an agent or work with him or her as a transaction broker.

3.A.14   What are an agent's duties and obligations?

Once an agency relationship is created, the licensee owes certain fiduciary duties to his or her client in addition to the basic duties previously listed. Generally, fiduciary duties require the placement of the client's interest ahead of the interests of any other party to the transaction.

Additionally, the New Mexico agent must also disclose to the client all information known by the licensee that is material to the transaction and that is not known to the client or could not be discovered by the client through a reasonably diligent inspection. The agent must also disclose any financial interests the brokerage has in the transaction. Finally, the New Mexico broker may not accept any fees from anyone other than his or her client or, with the principal's consent, the other party to the transaction.

In New Mexico, the agent is obligated to place the client's interest ahead of the interest of any other party *(loyalty)*, unless to do so violates the law. The agent must fulfill the instructions *(obedience)* within the scope of the agency agreement (unless they are unlawful instructions).

When a seller's agent uses his or her superior skill to help the seller arrive at a realistic listing price, develop a marketing plan, and negotiate offers, *reasonable care* is demonstrated. A buyer's agent demonstrates reasonable care by helping the buyer evaluate property values, financial alternatives, offers, and counteroffers.

The duty of *accounting* requires the recording and reporting of all funds received from or on behalf of the principal. State law requires that these funds be deposited into the broker's trust account immediately after the date on the document identifying receipt of the last signature of acceptance. Obviously, as mentioned earlier, unlawful *commingling* is illegal (see 2.C.8). (*Conversion* is the illegal practice of spending commingled funds for personal use.)

B. Brokerage Relationship Disclosures

3.B.1   What is brokerage relationship disclosure?

When working with consumers in a real estate transaction, New Mexico law requires that licensees provide written basic licensee duties disclosures. The written disclosure form, signed by the client, verifies that the licensee has, in fact, discussed basic licensee duties with the client. The disclosure must include a list of the licensee's basic duties and any conflicts of interest, and additionally a licensee must disclose any written brokerage relationship with another party to the transaction. The basic licensee duties include honesty and reasonable skill, care, and diligence; assistance throughout the transaction (unless written instructions to the contrary are given); and disclosure of adverse material facts actually known. A complete list of these duties can be found in the Commission rules 16 NMAC 61.19.

3.B.2   At what time must the disclosure be made?

The initial disclosure must be in writing and made prior to the time a licensee generates or presents any document with the potential to become an express written agreement (contract).

3.B.3   What are some examples of express written agreements?

Listing agreements, buyer–broker agreements, purchase agreements, management agreements, leases, and letters of intent are some examples of express written agreements. An express written agreement is any document signed by all parties to the transaction.

3.B.4   When is the disclosure made?

The time frame varies, depending on whether the client is a seller, buyer, landlord, or tenant.

Thus, the licensee discloses with a seller before a listing agreement is signed. Buyers must acknowledge in writing the disclosure before a buyer–broker agreement is signed or an offer is made, and sellers must receive the disclosure before an offer is presented. The form is kept on file in the listing broker's office and the buyer's broker's office for three years.

3.B.5   Does the basic licensee duties disclosure include agreements for broker compensation?

No. The consumer's agreement to compensate a licensee is determined by a brokerage agreement, not by a disclosure. The existence of a written agreement with another party to the transaction must be disclosed, as would any compensation to be received from that other party.

3.B.6   Does the basic licensee duties disclosure create any obligations on the part of the buyer or seller?

The disclosure is simply an acknowledgment that basic licensee duties have been discussed with the consumer. The consumer should sign the document as "proof" that the licensee has made the required disclosure. Thus, the buyer or seller is still free to work with other agents.

What is critical is that the disclosure does set obligations on the part of the licensee-agent. Written authority to provide real estate services may be obtained at this time, but it is not required, unless the client chooses to have those services provided in an agency relationship.

3.B.7   What about dual agency disclosures?

Offices may have a policy permitting dual agency with informed written consent. In a dual agency, the licensee must endeavor to remain impartial and not aggressively represent the interest of either party to the exclusion or detriment of the other party. Licensees can act as dual agents only if all parties give their written consent in the form of a separate written dual agency agreement.

The possibility of dual agency should be discussed and agreed on before the seller signs a listing agreement or before providing specific assistance to the buyer. If the consumer creates an agency agreement with the agent and agrees to the possibility of dual agency, then a second disclosure is required at the time that the agent actually becomes a dual agent.

3.B.8   What happens if no basic licensee duties disclosure is made?

Failure to disclose in writing before the consumer enters an express written agreement is a prima facie violation of license law and rules, and the licensee is subject to disciplinary action. However, a failure to disclose does not affect the validity of title to real property already transferred.

3.B.9   Are any other disclosures required?

Unless a written notice to the contrary exists, licensees are prohibited from accepting undisclosed compensation (related to a transaction) from any person other than the agreed parties. Also, licensees must disclose in writing when acting in a transaction on their own behalf, on behalf of an immediate family member or brokerage, or on behalf of a business entity in which the licensee has an interest.

C. Brokerage Agreements

3.C.1   What is brokerage?

A real estate broker is defined as a person licensed to buy, sell, exchange, auction, deal in options, lease real property, or offer to do so for others and to charge a fee for those services. As discussed in Chapter 1, New Mexico requires a license to act as a broker, advertise one's services as a broker, negotiate, collect rents, or seek out prospects for real estate-related activities.

3.C.2   What are brokerage agreements?

Brokerage agreements are essentially employment contracts requesting the professional services of the licensee, not the transfer of real estate. Brokerages enter into employment agreements with sellers, with buyers, with landlords, and with tenants. Brokerage agreements confirm compensation issues and determine the brokerage relationship.

Depending on the agreement, the broker could be an agent or a principal.

In a listing agreement, the seller is the principal (client), and the broker delegates the work to his agents (affiliate licensees). In a brokerage agreement with a buyer, the buyer is the principal (client), and the broker delegates the work to his or her affiliates.

The employment agreement will also determine if the broker is to be an agent or transaction broker of the buyer or seller principal. In many firms, the broker will choose designated agency, appointing a licensee(s) as exclusive representative of the principal client.

3.C.3 Are referral fees legal in New Mexico?

Every year real estate licensees help thousands of families by referring them to other licensees across the United States. In return for the referral, a percentage or other agreed-on fee is paid to the referring broker. These fees are legal if paid between brokers.

3.C.4 What are the brokerage agreements between the brokerage and consumers?

A brokerage agreement sets forth the rights and obligations of both parties and generally includes an agreement for broker compensation. These agreements are entered into by the brokerage with sellers, buyers, tenants, and landlords. The rules are the same whether the real estate is residential, commercial, industrial, or special-purpose.

3.C.5 What are the various brokerage employment agreements with consumers?

A seller hires a broker under a **listing agreement.** An agreement between a broker and a buyer is a **buyer brokerage agreement. A management agreement** is a contract between a property owner and the broker who is hired to manage the rental property.

Even if an affiliate associate broker negotiates the agreement, the contract is still between the consumer and the broker. It is important to remember that the brokerage relationship disclosure merely acknowledges disclosure; the aforementioned agreements address the brokerage relationship chosen, exclusivity, and compensation issues.

3.C.6 What are exclusive listings?

Exclusive-right-to-sell listing agreements give brokerage firms the exclusive right to market the seller's property and receive a commission during the term of the listing, regardless of which person sells it, including the owner. A variation is the **exclusive-agency** listing, in which the owner of the property promises to compensate the broker for locating a buyer, but the owner reserves the right to produce the buyer without paying the broker a commission. New Mexico Statutes state that the listing agreement must clearly state if the agreement is an exclusive agency or an exclusive right to sell.

3.C.7   What is a net listing and can New Mexico brokers take net listings?

A net listing is an agreement that specifies a net sale price to be received by the owner with the excess over that price to be received by the broker as commission. This situation presents a potential conflict of interest for the broker.

Often, the seller realizes the true value of the property only when an offer to purchase is obtained. Because of the possibility of a conflict of interest between the broker-client relationship and the broker's profit motive, the taking of a net listing should be done with great care and with full disclosure.

3.C.8   What specifically must a listing agreement include?

To have legal recognition, all listing contracts in New Mexico must be written. The listing agreement should properly identify the property and the terms and conditions under which the property is to be sold.

Specifically, the listing agreement should include the listing price and the commission to be paid. The signatures of all parties are required, and a definite expiration date is required on all exclusive listings. As stated in 3.C.6, the agreement must specify exclusivity. Licensees are required to give a legible copy of the agreement to the owner as soon as reasonably practicable after the listing agreement has been signed by the owner(s).

3.C.9   At what time may a listing broker place a For Sale sign on the property?

It is illegal to place a sign on any property offering it for sale, rent, or lease without the owner's consent. Thus, the broker may place the sign whenever the seller agrees. Many brokerages include specific authorization for a For Sale sign as part of the listing agreement.

3.C.10   Who or what determines the brokerage fee?

Any commission or fee in any brokerage agreement is fully negotiable among the parties to that brokerage agreement. The listing contract must spell out the broker's commission rate. It can be either a percentage of the sale or a flat fee. The seller, in the listing contract, may authorize the listing company to share compensation with other licensees, including a buyer's agent solely representing the buyer.

Once the parties to a brokerage agreement agree on the structure of the commission, no party other than the listing broker is allowed to alter or attempt to alter the commission arrangement without the prior written consent of the seller and listing broker.

3.C.11   What is procuring cause?

Procuring cause in a real estate transaction means that a licensee started or caused a chain of events that resulted in the sale of a listed property. Procuring cause disputes generally occur between cooperative brokers and are normally settled by arbitration through local boards or associations. The Commission specifically does not have jurisdiction over disputes between brokers as to fees and commissions.

3.C.12   Are there any other considerations that may be included in a listing agreement?

The agreement should address any reserved items and, if agreed on, a protection clause. In addition, permission must be given for the installation of a lockbox for purposes of ingress and egress, and permission must be obtained to place a For Sale sign. Authorization is required if the listing is going to be shared through a multiple-listing service.

3.C.13   Who must sign a listing agreement?

To have a valid listing agreement, everyone who has an ownership interest should sign the listing agreement.

3.C.14   What is a protection clause, and whom does it protect?

At the present time, the use of protection clauses in a brokerage agreement is not specifically addressed in New Mexico law. However, if the broker does include such a clause, it is presumed that the clause would have to be part of the original agreement. The clause would have to include a definite protection time frame.

A **protection clause** protects the broker from unscrupulous sellers or buyers who take the broker's generated leads and then buy or sell the property *after the brokerage agreement expires* to avoid paying a commission to the broker. A protection clause can be included in either the listing or buyer brokerage agreement and extends beyond the expiration of the agreement.

For listings, before the expiration of the listing agreement, the broker should furnish to the owner the names and addresses of the persons to whom the property was presented during the active term of the listing and for whom protection is sought. If the seller enters into a contract to sell the property to one of these buyers during the protected time period, the seller owes the broker a commission.

For buyer brokerage agreements, the clause would state that at the expiration of the agreement, if the buyer purchases, leases, or acquires any interest in any property previously shown by the licensee, the buyer agrees to pay an agreed-on fee. The licensee would have to submit to the buyer, prior to the expiration of the agreement, a list of the sellers' names, addresses, and property addresses for which protection is sought.

3.C.15   Can a broker solicit another broker's listing?

Legally binding listing agreements must be respected by outside parties. Alienating those involved in contractual relationships is illegal.

From time to time, a seller who is under contract with a broker may contact a second broker and want to discuss listing with the second broker. The second broker may talk with a seller who initiates the call. However, any listing entered into before the expiration of a valid listing may subject the seller to liability for double commissions.

3.C.16   Can a broker assign a listing to another broker?

Listing agreements may not be assigned, sold, or otherwise transferred to another broker without the express written consent of all the parties to the original agreement.

3.C.17   Is it legal for a licensee who decides to work for a different broker to transfer listings to the new brokerage?

On termination of employment, licensees are not allowed to take or use any written brokerage agreements secured during their employment with the first broker. Brokerage agreements are the property of the qualifying broker and can be canceled only by the broker and the seller, unless the terms of the contract state otherwise.

3.C.18   What does the brokerage agreement with a buyer have to include?

New Mexico Rules do not specifically address additional terms of a buyer brokerage agreement. However, for legal recognition and to be enforceable, all buyer brokerage agreements must be in writing. If the relationship is to be exclusive then the agreement must so state. The agreement should contain statements disclosing the brokerage policy (if any) on cooperating with and compensating other brokerages. Additionally, the duties and responsibilities of the buyer-client and the broker-licensee should be spelled out. Compensation issues should be addressed.

Besides this buyer-client, other potential buyers that the licensee is working with may be interested in the same property. The brokerage agreement terms should clarify under what circumstances the buyer's representative may deal with those other buyers regardless if the situation arises before, during, or after the end of the contract. Also, the licensee should not disclose to any buyer the terms of another's offer. The agreement should discuss methods of contacting competing buyers.

The licensee should ask the buyer to acknowledge that the licensee is acting solely as a licensee, and not as an attorney, tax adviser, lender, appraiser, surveyor, structural engineer, property inspector, consultant, or other professional adviser. Buyers are advised to seek professional advice concerning the condition of the property, status of title, and other legal and tax matters concerning any proposed transaction.

3.C.19   Can a buyer's brokerage agreement be assigned or sold to another broker?

Unless the terms of the agreement state otherwise, buyer brokerage contracts cannot be assigned, sold, or otherwise transferred to another broker without the express written consent of all parties to the original agreement.

3.C.20   Can the licensee take buyer brokerage agreements to a second broker?

On termination, licensees are not allowed to take or use any written buyer brokerage agreements secured during their employment. These agreements remain the property of the qualifying broker and may be canceled only by the broker and the buyer-client.

3.C.21   Does the licensee owe the buyer-client anything after the termination of the relationship?

Legal and ethical implications of agency survive even after the termination of a buyer's agreement. Other responsibilities include accounting for monies and property related to and received during the contractual period, as well as keeping confidentially requested information confidential.

3.C.22   Under what circumstances may a qualifying broker (or his or her affiliated licensees) meet another broker's client?

Listing licensees usually allow a buyer's representative to accompany prospects at any step in a real estate transaction, except a listing licensee is not required to permit a buyer's agent to be present when presenting an offer to a seller-client or discussing confidential matters with the seller-client. With the listing licensee present, sometimes buyer's representatives are afforded the courtesy to personally present their client's purchase offer directly to the seller. If this courtesy is not extended, the buyer's representative presents the buyer's purchase offer to the listing licensee and the listing licensee (singularly) then presents the offer to the seller.

3.C.23   Do brokers have to cooperate with and compensate each other?

Brokers recognize that while one brokerage has the listing, another broker may already be working with a buyer. The buyer wants to continue to work with his own licensee, not the listing brokerage. In this situation, the seller benefits from the listing broker's agreeing to share the compensation with the broker who actually procures the buyer. This cooperation benefits the seller by presenting the property to more potential buyers.

New Mexico law does not require that a broker cooperate with or compensate another broker. However, the listing agreement should include a statement disclosing the brokerage policy on cooperating with and compensating other brokerages. The listing agreement must address whether the brokerage can appoint subagents or act as a dual agent, including whether the brokerage intends to share the commission with another brokerage. This disclosure is intended to inform the client of any policy that would limit the participation of any other brokerage.

3.C.24   What kind of agreement exists between a qualifying broker and the people who work for the broker?

Qualifying brokers enter into employment agreements with the licensees who work for them. Such agreements permit licensees to act as agents for their qualifying brokers. Thus, even though an affiliated licensee may obtain the listing or buyer brokerage agreement, the agreement is in the name of the broker. In the employment contract with affiliate licensees, the broker is the principal and the affiliate licensees are the broker's agents.

A qualifying broker is responsible for supervising the real estate activities performed by an associate broker employed by or otherwise associated with the broker as the broker's representative, even if the affiliated licensee is classified as an independent contractor. The associate broker is responsible for keeping the qualifying broker fully informed of all activities being conducted on behalf of the broker and any other activities that might affect the broker's responsibilities.

In New Mexico, the broker who fails to properly supervise the activities of an associated licensee is subject to disciplinary action. The broker is responsible for the associate's activities, even if the associate does not keep the broker fully informed.

Unless the broker was not properly supervising the licensee, the broker generally is not held responsible for an affiliated licensee's actions if the broker had no guilty knowledge of the licensee's actions.

3.C.25   Is there anything else to know regarding brokerage agreements?

The licensee must keep confidential information confidential, even after the brokerage agreement is terminated.

D. Property Management Agreements

3.D.1   What is a management contract?

A **management contract** is between the brokerage and the owner of rental property who wishes to lease real property but does not want to deal directly with tenants and the property. The owner hires a brokerage to "manage" the property; that is, locate tenants, handle repairs, collect rents, and so forth. New Mexico rules require that this contract for a broker's services be in writing.

In New Mexico, if a licensee wants to become a property owner's authorized leasing agent, a disclosure of basic licensees duties must be made prior to generating the contract. A current written agreement is required to be on file with the licensee's qualifying broker. Written property management agreements or comparable written authorizations signed by the owner or the owner's authorized agent are required before any brokerage is allowed to represent the owner of the property.

3.D.2   What must be included in the management agreement?

First, the agreement must specify whether the property will be operated in the name of the owner or the brokerage. The manager and owner should spell out the structure of their relationship, their specific responsibilities and liabilities, the scope of the manager's authority, fees, and the duration of the management agreement. Property managers generally have broad ongoing authority as general agents. While New Mexico law does not go into greater detail, property management agreements should include a proper identification of the property, all the terms and conditions under which the property is to be managed, and the powers and authority given to the broker by the owner. The terms and conditions under which the broker is to remit property income and when periodic written statements of property income and expense are to be forwarded for owner review must also be included.

Additionally, the management agreement should address the following:

- Authorization for payments to third parties
- Broker's compensation for services rendered
- Required dollar amounts for security deposits
- An effective date of the agreement
- Terms and conditions for termination of the property management agreement
- Signatures of the broker and owner or authorized representative

3.D.3   How are the owner's funds treated?

The qualifying broker is required to deposit all funds received on behalf of the owner into the qualifying broker's trust account as soon after receipt as practicably possible. Management fees may be withdrawn from the owner's account when the basis for computation can be determined, in accordance with the management agreement. When withdrawn, the funds are deposited into the broker's business operating account. The qualifying broker must always create a paper trail.

As previously mentioned (see 2.C.17), the qualifying broker who manages six or more individual units is required to maintain a separate property management trust account.

E.   Antitrust Laws

3.E.1   Does New Mexico have an antitrust law?

No. At the present time, New Mexico operates under several federal laws. The Sherman Antitrust Act prohibits any contract or conspiracy to restrain interstate or foreign trade. It also prohibits monopolies. The federal Clayton Act regulates unethical practices that may be harmful to fair competition. In real estate, harmful practices include boycotting, price-fixing, and tying agreements.

4 Contracts and Closings Overview

When preparing to make and accept offers for the sale or rental of real property, buyers and sellers want to make decisions based on full knowledge of the property and title. Additionally, in today's marketplace, the real estate industry has seen a movement from *caveat emptor (buyer beware)* to *seller disclose.* Today, sellers are asked to disclose information material to a buyer making an informed decision. Seller property condition disclosure forms are customary in most New Mexico markets, but are not required by law.

The New Mexico Real Estate Commission has addressed these concerns. This chapter discusses contract issues including offers and acceptances, fraud, closing concerns, stigmatized properties, and certain environmental topics.

A. Contract Issues

4.A.1 What is a contract?

A **contract** is a set of legally binding promises between two informed parties that must be performed and for which, if a breach occurs, the law provides a remedy. For legal recognition, everything related to the transfer of New Mexico real estate must be in writing. In addition, any agreement for a fee must be in writing (47-1-45 NMSA 1978) or the agreement is void.

In New Mexico, on execution of any instrument in connection with a real estate transaction, licensees are required as soon as practicable to deliver legible copies of the original document to all parties. It is the responsibility of the licensee to prepare sufficient copies of such instruments to satisfy this requirement. The statute of limitations for contractual matters is six years in New Mexico.

4.A.2   What is the age of legal competence in New Mexico, with no exceptions, to enter a contract?

In New Mexico a person is legally competent at age 18.

4.A.3   What does informed parties mean?

Before entering into a legally binding contract to buy or sell real estate, what the parties offer and accept must be the same. Hence, it is important that sellers disclose every important issue affecting the property. Otherwise, the buyer is buying less than agreed on. It is an act of fraud to intentionally withhold disclosure of material adverse facts. This is called *passive fraud.* Sometimes, a seller or licensee does not know and negligently withholds information. In these situations, the buyer may be able to void the contract.

4.A.4   What is an adverse material fact?

In New Mexico, adverse **material facts** are those conditions or occurrences that are generally recognized or specifically stated by the purchaser to be of such significance that they would affect either party's decision to enter into a contract. Included in this definition are those situations that significantly and adversely affect the value of a property and those situations that significantly reduce the structural integrity of a property. Also, any situation that presents a significant health risk to the occupants of the property would be considered an adverse material fact.

4.A.5   What is fraud?

Fraudulent acts require *intentional* deception in such a way as to harm another person. Included in the definition are fraudulent advertising, making false statements about a property's condition, and intentionally concealing known facts (passive fraud). Such fraudulent acts subject a licensee to license suspension or revocation.

4.A.6   What is negligence?

Misrepresentation or omission of pertinent facts does not have to be intentional to bring liability exposure. **Negligence** occurs when licensees *should have known* that incorrect statements were being relied on as material fact.

4.A.7   Who is permitted to draw up contracts for the purchase or lease of real estate?

New Mexico does not have any statutory guidance. While there is no law, the accepted standard is from a document called "Statement of Principles," prepared by the REALTORS® and the Bar Association. Essentially, licensees are not permitted to draft contracts, but rather to use preprinted contracts by filling in blanks. Attorneys must prepare these contracts.

New Mexico does not have Commission-promulgated forms. Most of the contracts used for residential and vacant land transactions are published by REALTOR® organizations or are prepared by attorneys.

4.A.8   What specifically may a broker NOT prepare?

In New Mexico, real estate brokers should be cautious to avoid the charge of practicing law without a license. Specifically, a licensee may not create estates in remainder or leases for periods greater than ten years. Brokers are not allowed to prepare legal documents; licensed attorneys must prepare these documents. A broker may fill in the blanks on forms prepared by attorneys.

4.A.9   How is real property described in New Mexico legal documents?

Land may be described using metes and bounds, lot and block, the U.S. Rectangular Survey, and/or the New Mexico Coordinate System. The New Mexico Coordinate System is a method of determining the point of beginning for a described parcel of real estate. The system uses a reference to an *xy* coordinate grid. If there is any conflict between the New Mexico and the U.S. systems, the U.S. system prevails.

4.A.10   Is a legal description required in a listing agreement?

New Mexico law does not specifically address this issue. However, there must be a *meeting of the minds* to make a contract, and the street address must be definitive enough to clarify what is being purchased. Street addresses are not generally considered legal descriptions because of their temporary nature. A street address in a listing agreement may be sufficient to locate the property but not to describe its boundaries. It is best that the legal description appear in an offer to purchase to be sure of a legally binding contract.

4.A.11   What forms must be completed during a real estate transaction?

In addition to the purchase agreement, New Mexico requires the use only of the Basic Licensee Duties Disclosure. Property disclosures are not required in New Mexico. However, a copy must be given to the purchaser if the seller has previously completed one. If the residence was built prior to 1978, the seller(s) and buyer(s) must sign the lead-based paint disclosure form.

New Mexico Commission rules require that every broker deliver to the seller a complete detailed closing statement and at the same time a detailed closing statement to the buyer. The broker must retain copies of these closing statements for three years after the date of closing, along with a copy of the listing, any offers to purchase, and all pertinent correspondence.

B. Residential Property Seller Disclosure Statement

4.B.1   What is the purpose of a property seller disclosure statement?

Although seller disclosure forms are not required by law to be used in New Mexico, REALTOR® organizations publish a number of Property Condition Disclosure Forms for different types of property.

The purpose of any property disclosure statement is to forewarn prospective buyers of the condition of the property before they write an offer. If the property is not as described, then the buyer may have grounds to revoke the offer. The disclosure statement includes information about the property's plumbing, electrical, and heating systems; any significant structural defects; presence of pests; zoning classification; and whether the property is in a real estate improvement district.

4.B.2   When must the property disclosure be made?

When a disclosure is requested, it is usually a contingency in the purchase offer. Sellers and licensees should use great care to ensure delivery of current and accurate information. Sellers, not licensees, should always make this disclosure.

4.B.3   How should these changes be handled if some items change after the seller filled out a property disclosure form?

Once the form is delivered, any new discoveries (like previous termite infestation) require an amended statement. If any items on the disclosure change during the escrow period, the form should be updated and delivered to the purchaser.

C.   Offers and Acceptances

4.C.1   Does the listing broker have to let the buyer's broker present the offer to the seller-client?

Listing brokers are not required to permit a buyer's broker to be present when presenting offers or discussing confidential matters with their seller-clients. However, in some New Mexico brokerage communities, it is customary to give buyers' brokers the privilege of presenting a buyer's offer.

4.C.2   In what order are multiple offers presented to the seller for consideration?

New Mexico Real Estate Commission rules state that any and all offers received must be promptly presented to the seller for consideration or the listing broker can face disciplinary action. The seller must be permitted to view all offers to determine which offer is best for him or her. The formal acceptance or rejection must then be promptly communicated to the prospective buyer or buyer's broker.

The licensee needs to help the buyer understand that another offer may be presented while the seller is considering the first offer. No particular courtesies are extended to the person writing the first offer. There is no particular advantage to writing the first offer.

4.C.3   Other offers arrive after the seller accepts an offer. Should the subsequent offers be presented?

The seller has the right to see offers that arrive, even if he or she has accepted an offer. The seller is still bound to the accepted offer but may wish to view a later offer as a possible backup or secondary offer. However, many listing agreements limit the licensee's duty to present offers after a contract has been signed. The seller cannot arbitrarily withdraw his acceptance and sell to another party.

4.C.4   Once the offer is accepted, what rights does the buyer have in the property?

After a purchase agreement is signed and the buyer or buyer's agent is in receipt of the signed document, equitable title passes to the purchaser. At this point, although the buyer has an insurable interest in the property, most contracts place the insurance burden on the seller during the escrow period. The

Vendor Purchaser Risk Act places the risk of loss on the seller, unless possession or legal title has transferred.

4.C.5   What is meant by "dual contracts" and why are they illegal in New Mexico?

The term **dual contracts** refers to two contracts from the same buyer on the same property. One of the offers is used *to purchase* the property while the other is used *to finance* the property. The offer to purchase can be either written or just an oral arrangement, while the offer to finance is generally written.

The true purchase price is known only between the contracting parties. The purpose of these contracts is to enable the buyer *to obtain a larger loan* than the true sale price or to enable the buyer *to qualify* for a loan that the buyer otherwise could not obtain. *Thus, the lender is deceived.* In New Mexico, any person who participates in these actions could be found guilty of a fraudulent practice and would be subject to disciplinary action.

D. Closings

4.D.1   Under what conditions can the buyer request that some funds be withheld from the seller until all of the repairs are completed?

Matters related to performance of the seller or buyer are most often legal judgments, requiring the professional expertise of an attorney. If a buyer demands the withholding of funds as a matter of right and refuses to perform unless the demand is met, the buyer may likewise be liable for failure to perform if his or her demand is not within the scope of the appropriate law governing the circumstances.

Real estate licensees should strongly urge their buyer-clients to consult with an attorney before making such demands. If, however, a buyer and seller freely negotiate the withholding of funds for repairs that are acknowledged by the seller to require completion, the real estate licensee can assist in the negotiation and request that an appropriate party hold an escrow. The wisest choice as an escrow agent is usually a title company that is familiar with these arrangements.

4.D.2   Who keeps copies of all of these documents and for how long?

At closing, the broker is required to keep copies of all executed documents for three years. The *seller's closing statement* shows all of the receipts and disbursements handled by the broker. The *buyer's closing statement* shows all monies received by the broker and how and for what they were disbursed.

4.D.3   Can brokers charge to prepare some documents?

According to the previously mentioned "Statement of Principles," real estate brokers cannot charge a fee for the preparation of purchase agreements and other documents related to closings.

E. Stigmatized Properties

4.E.1   What is a stigmatized property?

A **stigmatized property** is one that has acquired an undesirable reputation. Stigmatized properties can include homes psychologically impacted by newsworthy incidents such as a murder or murder/suicide, properties suspected of being a front for illegal drug sales, or properties that were the site of a forcible felony.

The New Mexico Real Estate Disclosure Act specifically addresses property that is the site of a natural death or the site of a homicide, suicide, assault, sexual assault, or any other crime punishable as a felony. Although such property may be stigmatized, there is no obligation on the part of the real estate licensee to discover or disclose these facts.

Under the federal fair housing laws, it is specifically illegal to disclose that a property is or has been owned and occupied by person who is HIV-positive or has AIDS. This includes any other disease that has been determined by medical evidence to be highly unlikely to be transmitted to others through the occupancy of improvements to real property.

4.E.2   Is there any responsibility for failure to disclose information about stigmatized property?

The essence of the issue is discovery, not disclosure. There is no duty for the seller or licensee to disclose such information.

Based on New Mexico statute, no cause of action is warranted against a licensee for failure to discover that the purchased property was *psychologically* impacted. However, if the licensee had prior knowledge, then, under an agency relationship, the buyer's agent may have a duty to disclose the known information.

Licensees must distinguish between a stigma and a potential adverse material fact. A drug lab is something that might create an adverse material fact as an environmental clean-up issue. The environmental hazard has nothing to do with the stigma, and would require disclosure.

F. Environmental Concerns

4.F.1 Who implements CERCLA in New Mexico?

The New Mexico Environment Department is the enforcement agency for the Comprehensive Environmental Response, Compensation, and Liability Act's (CERCLA) *Superfund and Uncontrolled Site Regulations in New Mexico.* This agency may be reached at 1190 Saint Francis Drive, Santa Fe, NM 87502-0110. The phone numbers are 505-827-2855 or 800-219-6157. The Web site address is *www.nmenv.state.nm.us.*

4.F.2 Who is responsible for cleaning up hazardous waste on a property?

Responsibility varies. Because cleanups can be quite costly, prospective buyers should certainly obtain as many reports as are available from the EPA, the New Mexico Environment Department, and even from private environmental specialists.

4.F.3 What state agency controls rights to water in New Mexico?

The New Mexico State Engineer and local conservancy districts control use and distribution of water. Water is scarce and valuable. Often irrigation and other water rights are as valuable or more valuable than the actual land to which they are attached. Within limits, water rights may be transferred. Permission to divert, store, or withdraw water must not be assumed.

4.F.4 Of what should the buyer be aware before building on an acreage and installing a septic system?

In New Mexico, county health officials monitor septic tanks and private sewage disposal systems. New Mexico allows the use of both aerobic and anaerobic systems. For proper drainage, the ground must be able to absorb the liquid waste. A percolation test is conducted that monitors the time that it takes water poured through a pipe to be absorbed by the soil. A permit may not be issued if there is insufficient absorption. Many counties today are placing very severe restrictions on private sewage systems due to ground water quality concerns. Licensees involved in a sale should confer with the appropriate authorities.

4.F.5   Are there other issues of which a developer should be aware?

All subdivisions must be developed in accordance with the subdivision act. Equally important is flood plain status according to FEMA maps. In addition, the New Mexico Cultural Properties Act limits the excavation or disturbance of archaeological or burial sites. There are numerous sites like this in New Mexico, and a survey must be done to determine if development is possible and at what cost.

4.F.6   Does New Mexico have a lead-based paint hazard reduction law?

New Mexico operates under the federal Title X Lead-Based Paint Poisoning Prevention Act, passed in 1992. This legislation requires notification of possible exposure to lead-based paint in all pre-1978 residential and apartment dwellings. In New Mexico, the EPA has jurisdiction over lead-based paint disclosure enforcement.

The seller is required to notify the buyer of any known lead-based hazards and provide the buyer with any information on lead-based hazards from risk assessments or inspections in the seller's possession. The seller must also provide a booklet to the buyer or tenant. Buyers (but not tenants) have the right to have the property inspected within ten days or any time period agreed on, or to waive this right. Failure to disclose any known presence is subject to a $10,000 fine per violation. Copies of these disclosures must be retained for three years.

4.F.7   Does New Mexico require any other disclosures of environmental presence, such as asbestos and UFFI?

No, New Mexico does not require any specific environmental disclosures. Radon testing is not required, but is a common part of residential real estate sales. New Mexico has a high incidence of natural uranium deposits.

G. Title Issues

4.G.1   Is New Mexico a title or lien-theory state?

New Mexico is a lien-theory state. This means that the owner-borrower gives the lender a mortgage lien to use as collateral instead of a deed. The owner-borrower signs a promissory note as evidence of the debt and signs a mortgage lien instrument as collateral for the debt. If the owner defaults on the loan, the lender can file for a judicial foreclosure on the property. In New Mexico, the owner-borrower never relinquishes legal title.

4.G.2 How does a buyer know that title to the property is "good and marketable"?

An abstractor or attorney examines the *recorded* history of the property, and this report is then given to the buyer's attorney for an *opinion*. Title defects discovered by the examination may then be corrected. The buyer can buy title insurance.

Once the buyer's attorney is satisfied that marketable title can be transferred, the lender proceeds with the closing. The deed is delivered, and legal title passes to the purchaser. Customarily, deeds are recorded before the financing company releases the borrower's funds.

H. Conveyance Taxes

4.H.1 Does New Mexico charge conveyance taxes?

No, New Mexico does not have any conveyance taxes.

5 License Law Enforcement Overview

This chapter covers how the New Mexico Real Estate Commission (NMREC) considers violations of license law or rule. Generally, after proper disciplinary hearings, NMREC exercises its control over licensees through public reprimands, reeducation, fines, and the denial, suspension, or revocation of licenses.

NMREC also requires an added protection to provide compensation to a consumer who suffers monetary damage as a result of a licensee's error or negligence. Each active licensee is required to purchase errors and omissions (E&O) insurance, which is similar to malpractice insurance.

A. License Law Enforcement

5.A.1 Is a violation of New Mexico license law a misdemeanor or a felony?

Most violations under New Mexico license law are considered misdemeanors. NMREC may refer a complaint against a nonlicensee before any court of competent jurisdiction and take necessary actions to enforce the law and collect penalties. Effective July 1, 2001, NMREC may impose a civil penalty in an amount not to exceed $1,000 for each violation of unlicensed activity.

5.A.2 Under what circumstances may the New Mexico Real Estate Commission investigate licensees?

The Commission is allowed to investigate the actions of any licensee on its own motion and/or on the receipt of a verified written complaint. The

Commission has a staff of in-house investigators. In connection with an investigation, the Commission is authorized by New Mexico law to subpoena books, papers, records, and even witnesses. The Real Estate Commission is given authority to conduct hearings, and if the licensee is found guilty, his or her license could be revoked or suspended. Witnesses who fail to cooperate may be found guilty of contempt of court.

5.A.3 What are some of the reasons that can trigger an investigation?

NMREC is charged with protecting the interests of the public. Consequently, the Commission has jurisdiction over actions by a licensee that can harm the consumer in a real estate transaction. A complaint filed by a member of the public or the Commission will trigger an investigation. The Commission also conducts routine inspections, which may uncover some violations.

The Commission may investigate a licensee's actions for any of the following reasons:

- Trust account discrepancies
- Fraudulent activities
- Substantial misrepresentations
- Undisclosed dual agency
- Accepting a commission as a licensee from anyone except the brokerage
- Representing two brokerages without the knowledge of both brokers
- A broker's failing to account for or remit monies into his or her trust account in a timely manner
- Paying a "birddog" fee (commission) to someone who is not licensed for real estate referrals
- Failing to provide requested information to the Real Estate Commission in a timely manner (within 14 days)
- Any other conduct that demonstrates deceit or professional incompetency

5.A.4 How does the Commission determine when and if to follow up on a complaint?

Normally, a written complaint is filed that includes the complainant's full name, address, and telephone number plus the same information about the respondent. The complainant must include a concise statement of the facts clearly and accurately apprising the Commission of the allegations against the respondent. The complaint can either be personally delivered or mailed to the Real Estate Commission for review.

If an investigation by the staff determines a possible violation, the information is presented to the Commission in the form of a complaint against a "Broker B," which sets forth the alleged violation in anonymous fashion. Based on this information, the Commission then decides whether to conduct a hearing or dismiss the complaint. If the Commission finds cause, a Notice of Contemplated Action (NCA) is issued, giving the licensee 20 days to request a hearing.

5.A.5   Under what circumstances may the Commission investigator decide not to take a complaint before the Commission?

If the Commission investigator determines that there was no probable cause that warrants discipline, a letter is sent and the case closed. Reasons for refusing to set a hearing include the triviality of the allegation, insufficient evidence, effort to solve on a local level, lack of clarity of the issue, and lack of jurisdiction.

Recall that the mission of the Commission is to protect the public. Thus, Commission rules do not authorize the Commission to consider or conduct hearings involving disputes over fees or commissions between cooperating brokers, affiliated licensees, and other brokers.

5.A.6   How does the Commission decide on holding a hearing?

In determining the appropriate action, the Commission considers not only the severity of the violation and the sufficiency of evidence but also the possibility that the problem could be better resolved by other means available to the parties, without Commission involvement. The Commission discusses the clarity of the laws and rules that support the alleged violation, the clarity of the Commission's jurisdiction, whether the violation is likely to recur, and the record of the licensee.

5.A.7   When does the Commission use an "informal" hearing? Is it required?

While no provision exists for an informal hearing, the Commission and a licensee often agree that a violation has been committed. The parties can then agree to some minor disciplinary action and remedial measures in lieu of holding a hearing. This is still recorded as a disciplinary action against the licensee.

5.A.8   Can the respondent request a different hearing date?

Written requests for a continuance may be considered prior to the scheduled hearing, except in the case of an unanticipated emergency.

5.A.9 How may testimony be taken before the hearing?

Testimony may be taken by deposition, compelling any involved party to appear and depose in the same manner as witnesses are compelled to appear and testify in civil cases.

5.A.10 What are the legal effects of the hearing and possible disciplinary actions?

The Commission's decision can exonerate the licensee or revoke, suspend, or possibly not renew the license. Other disciplinary actions include probation, additional education or training, or issuing a citation and warning. A civil penalty may also be assessed: up to $500 and/or six months imprisonment for individuals and up to $1,000 for corporations.

5.A.11 What happens if the respondent does not appear?

The hearing will be held without the licensee. The licensee will be bound by the decision as if he or she had been there. In other words, the licensee loses the right to cross-examine witnesses and to present a defense. In most cases, failure to appear will cause the revocation of the license by default. A licensee does not have the right to appeal the default to District Court.

5.A.12 Is there any possibility of an appeal?

The Commission must hold hearings in accordance with the Uniform Licensing Act (ULA). The parties to the hearing process may agree to toll the statute of limitations in certain circumstances. ULA outlines the appeal process. Appeals are made to District Court within 30 days of the Commission decision.

5.A.13 Is there anything else?

The Commission is required to follow the Criminal Offenders Employment Act in all denials of licenses or other disciplinary matters.

B. Suspended or Revoked Licenses

5.B.1 What are the immediate effects of a suspended or revoked qualifying broker's license?

A suspended or revoked license must be returned to the Commission, and as of the effective date, engaging in activities requiring a license is prohibited.

Note, though, that during the penalized period a licensee with a suspended or revoked license is allowed to receive compensation earned prior to the effective date of the suspension or revocation.

The revocation of the qualifying broker's (brokerage) license automatically suspends every license held by the broker by virtue of the licensee's employment. These licensees may return to real estate activities only when "hired" by another qualifying broker.

5.B.2 What are the effects on brokerage agreements when the qualifying broker's license is suspended or revoked?

On receipt of the Commission's order, the qualifying broker whose license has been suspended or revoked must cease all activities, including listings, buyer broker agreements, and property management agreements. The seller or lessor must be apprised of this. Assignments of listings or management agreements require written authorization of the seller or lessor.

A qualifying broker whose license has been suspended or revoked may not finalize any pending closings. With written approval of the concerned parties, this task may be delegated to a new qualifying broker who will handle the trust funds and close the transaction.

All advertising must cease. Qualifying brokers whose licenses have been suspended or revoked are prohibited from advertising real estate in any manner as a broker or answering their business telephones in any manner that might indicate that the brokerage is active in the real estate business.

5.B.3 Is the qualifying broker disciplined if one of his or her licensees is disciplined?

Any unlawful act or violation by a licensee is not cause for the revocation of the qualifying broker's license unless the qualifying broker had *guilty knowledge* of the unlawful act or Commission violation or failed to adequately supervise the transaction. Note, though, that during the penalized period a licensee with a suspended or revoked license is allowed to receive compensation earned prior to the effective date of the suspension or revocation.

C. Errors and Omissions Insurance

5.C.1   Does New Mexico have a recovery fund for victims?

New Mexico has a state recovery fund administered by the Real Estate Commission. Any party with an unpaid judgment against a licensee may file for recovery. The judgment must be based on fraud, knowing or willful misrepresentation, or conversion of funds resulting from a licensed activity. The claimant must file an appropriate petition within one year of the termination of all proceedings. Claims are limited to $10,000 per judgment and $30,000 per licensee. In addition, mandatory E&O insurance may provide some "injured party" recovery funds.

5.C.2   Are New Mexico licensees required to obtain bonding or errors and omissions insurance?

New Mexico law does not require that licensees be bonded. All active licensees must have E&O insurance. E&O insurance does not cover acts of fraud, only true errors or omissions.

5.C.3   What is errors and omissions insurance?

E&O insurance is a type of coverage that protects qualifying brokers and affiliated licensees from loss due to errors, mistakes, and negligence. New Mexico law requires that all active licensees carry E&O insurance. Licensees must submit evidence of compliance. The Commission is authorized to place licenses on inactive status if the E&O coverage lapses.

NMREC contracts with an insurance provider for a group policy that is made available to all licensees. The coverage contains a provision prohibiting the provider from canceling a licensee's coverage, except for nonpayment of premiums. The law allows licensees the option to obtain independent coverage, as long as the coverage meets the minimum standards adopted by the Real Estate Commission. The standards adopted by the Commission include minimum liability limits, permissible deductible limits, and permissible exceptions to the E&O coverage. Equivalent private coverage is also acceptable. Licensees may not self-insure.

The Commission offers a group policy through the contract carrier. The maximum premium is set by statute at $200 per year. Coverage is $100,000 per claim and $500,000 aggregate and includes first-dollar coverage for attorney fees (no deductible). There is a $1,000 deductible per covered claim, and the policy is cancelable only for nonpayment.

5.C.4 Must inactive licensees also carry E&O insurance?

No, individuals whose licenses are on inactive status with NMREC are not required to carry E&O insurance.

5.C.5 When must the E&O insurance be activated?

E&O insurance is a condition for licensure. Should an inactive license become active, the E&O insurance requirement would become applicable.

6 Specialty Topics

Many other professions and issues touch real estate brokerage. This chapter discusses appraisal requirements, landlord–tenant activities, and forms of ownership recognized in New Mexico.

A. Related Real Estate Activities

6.A.1 What are New Mexico state requirements for appraisers?

Appraisers must be licensed in New Mexico. The enforcement agency is the New Mexico Appraisers Board, located on the Web at *www.rld.state.nm.us/b&c/real_estate_appraisers_board.htm.* Mail may be sent to New Mexico Appraisers Board, 2055 South Pacheco Street, Suite 300, Santa Fe, NM 87504. Phone: 505-476-7096.

There are four levels of licensed appraisers in New Mexico:

1. **Registration** is the initial level for most appraisers when they have completed prelicensing education requirements. Once registered, candidates gain the appraisal experience that allows them to license at a higher level.
2. State-certified **general real estate appraiser.** To obtain this classification, the appraiser must present evidence of a minimum of 3,000 hours of appraisal experience over a period of not less than 30 months. At least 50 percent of the work must be nonresidential.
3. State-certified **residential real estate appraiser.** To achieve this classification, the appraiser must present evidence of a minimum of 2,500 hours of appraisal experience over at least 24 months.

4. State-licensed **real estate appraiser.** This category requires 2,000 hours of appraisal experience.

The Appraisal Foundation adopts changes in the real property appraiser qualification criteria from time to time. To obtain a copy of the current federal Uniform Standards of Professional Appraisal Practice from the Appraisal Foundation's Web site, use *www.appraisalfoundation.org.*

6.A.2   Do home inspectors have to be licensed?

At the present time, there is no requirement for licensing home inspectors.

B. Forms of Ownership

6.B.1   What forms of ownership are recognized in New Mexico?

New Mexico does not recognize tenancy by the entireties. It does recognize tenancy in common, joint tenancy, and community property.

6.B.2   Are dower and curtesy recognized in New Mexico?

No, dower and curtesy are not recognized in New Mexico.

6.B.3   What is separate and community property?

New Mexico is a community property state. This is important to married people. **Separate property** is property owned prior to marriage and includes property received during the marriage by gift or inheritance.

Community property is property acquired by a husband or wife during marriage from the earnings of either spouse. Community property is owned in equal undivided interests, no matter how much each spouse contributed.

C. Other Forms of Property Ownership

6.C.1   What about partnerships, corporations, and so forth?

The New Mexico Public Regulation Commission regulates all artificial entities in New Mexico. Real estate brokerages in New Mexico may include sole proprietorships, partnerships, limited liability company (LLC) operations, corporations, and subchapter S corporations. New Mexico law allows for the formation of single-person LLCs.

6.C.2   What are time-shares? Do they have to be registered?

Time-shares are a form of ownership interest that includes the use of a property for a fixed or variable period of time. The New Mexico Real Estate Commission has jurisdiction over time-share registration. Developers must register the project and pay $20 per unit, up to a maximum of $1,500.

6.C.3   What law covers time-shares?

The New Mexico Timeshare Act is 47-11-1 et. seq. NMSA 1978.

6.C.4   Does a time-share salesperson require a real estate license?

Any person engaged in the business or occupation of selling time-share estates for a fee or commission is required to obtain a real estate license. "Substantial" owners, defined as holding at least a 15 percent interest, are exempt from licensing requirements.

If a licensee is involved in selling time-shares that are deemed to be investment contracts, the licensee must follow securities laws.

6.C.5   Under what circumstances may a time-share purchaser rescind his or her contract?

There is a cooling-off period. A purchaser may at any time within seven business days following the receipt of all required information rescind in writing the contract of sale without stating any reason and without liability on the purchaser's part. All payments made before the decision to rescind must be refunded.

6.C.6   What is the difference between a condo and a co-op?

Cooperatives and condominiums are examples of multiple owners of the same property. Articles of incorporation, bylaws, definitions, and restrictive covenants are all different, and, therefore, due diligence is required before making a decision to purchase. The licensee who assists buyers in buying either type of property should always insist that the buyer read all relevant documents before entering into a purchase agreement.

Condo buyers receive a deed to real property. Co-op buyers receive personal property in the form of shares of stock inseparable from the proprietary leases.

6.C.7   What New Mexico laws govern cooperative and condominium ownership?

In a **cooperative,** the association or corporation owns the property. The Building Unit Ownership Act governs cooperative housing. By purchasing shares in the cooperative, the purchaser becomes an owner-tenant. The real estate is taxed in the name of the cooperative, but the individual owner-tenants are allowed to take tax deductions for the individual amounts paid as well as the same homestead tax credit and exemption as afforded individual property owners.

In **condominium** ownership, the individual dwelling owner is individually taxed. The Condominium Act covers condominium housing. It is important to remember that condominium is a form of ownership, not a style of building. Condo ownership is not limited to residential units; office buildings can also be condominium-owned.

There are different forms of condo ownership. Purchasers can own the *interior surfaces* of the unit, while the association owns the exterior and the grounds. In New Mexico, some condominium associations own the interior surfaces and the exterior. In other cases, such as a condominium town house, individual owners can own both the interior surfaces and the exterior.

6.C.8   How are unpaid association dues collected?

Note that all sums (association dues) assessed by the council of co-owners but unpaid for the share of the common expenses chargeable to any unit constitute a lien and can be foreclosed on by suit from the council of co-owners or the association management company representing the co-owners. In other words, as a form of protest, nonpayment of association dues is not a good idea.

D. Landlord–Tenant Issues

6.D.1   What New Mexico law covers landlord-tenant relations?

The Owner Resident Relations Act (47-8-1 et seq. NMSA 1978) applies to all rental residential dwellings in New Mexico. This chapter is designed to simplify, clarify, modernize, and revise the laws governing the rental of dwelling units and the rights and obligations of both landlords and tenants and encourage them to maintain and improve the quality of housing. In addition, the law ensures that the right to the receipt of rent is inseparable from the duty to maintain the premises.

Anyone who manages even one unit should have a copy of this law and consult it frequently. The days have gone by when the landlord or manager could simply change the locks and toss the tenant's belongings into the street. Today, the tenant has enforceable rights, and if the landlord violates these rights, the landlord may be faced with financial penalties.

6.D.2   Do all leases have to be in writing?

To receive legal recognition in the judicial system, New Mexico law requires that all lease agreements be in writing.

6.D.3   Are there any special clauses or items of which to be aware?

After the tenancy begins, the landlord must give a 24-hour written notice before entering the property, except in emergencies. If the tenant has requested repairs, the landlord can enter without such notice.

Rent is payable without notice or demand, and unless agreed otherwise is payable at the dwelling unit.

6.D.4   What if the landlord does not comply with the lease terms?

After a written seven-day notice by the tenant, if the landlord fails to initiate repairs and the unit is partially unusable or if the landlord otherwise violates the rental agreement, the tenant may abate up to one third of the monthly rent. If the unit cannot be occupied, the tenant may vacate and abate 100 percent of the rent for the time the property was unusable.

6.D.5   What specific procedures must a landlord follow to evict a tenant?

To evict a tenant, legal notice has to be given, and a judge decides whether the eviction action is appropriate.

6.D.6   For what reasons may a landlord terminate a rental agreement?

A landlord may terminate a rental agreement with proper notice for any of the following reasons:

- Nonpayment of rent
- Failure to comply with building codes affecting health and safety
- Failure to comply with the rental agreement
- Substantial violation

The tenant may terminate a rental agreement for a landlord's failure to comply with building codes affecting health and safety or failure to comply with the rental agreement.

6.D.7   How much notice must the landlord give to evict a tenant?

There are several different notice periods, depending on the circumstances. The landlord must give three days' notice for nonpayment, and seven days' notice is required for any other breach by either party. If the condition is corrected within the notice period, the tenancy continues.

In the case of a substantial violation, the landlord can give a three-day notice, terminating the rental agreement in three days without the opportunity to "correct" the problem. A substantial violation occurs when the tenant has committed a felony or assault, including drug use and property damage.

6.D.8   How may notice be served?

Notice may be given by personal service, by posting the notice on the tenant's door, or by U.S. mail. If the landlord chooses posting, he or she must also mail a copy of the notice.

6.D.9   How may a landlord regain possession from a holdover tenant?

Sometimes a tenant does not surrender the premises at the termination of the rental agreement. In this case, the landlord may file a petition for restitution with the magistrate court.

The court issues a summons, and a trial date is set for not less than seven nor more than ten days from the date of petition. The tenant may raise all defenses allowed in equity.

If the decision is in favor of the landlord, the judge will issue a writ of execution not later than seven days from the date of trial. The sheriff executes the writ and restores possession to the landlord. If the decision is in favor of the tenant, the tenancy continues.

The landlord has a duty to store the tenant's property for three days when the termination was for nonpayment, 30 days when termination is by abandonment (absence of the tenant without notice for more than seven days after rent is delinquent), and 14 days if termination is by surrender.

Prevailing parties can collect attorney fees. A landlord who does not act in good faith can be subject to a civil penalty of $250 and up to two times the monthly rental amount.

6.D.10   What are the requirements for holding a security deposit (for example, type of account, interest, limits on use, repayment)?

Landlords may charge a deposit of up to one month's rent on agreements of less than one year and do not have to pay any interest. If the agreement is for a year or more, the landlord must pay passbook interest on any deposit exceeding one month's rental amount. The broker must hold deposits in a trust account unless a written agreement exists allowing the deposit to be transferred to the owner.

The security deposit, along with an itemized accounting of any deductions, must be delivered or mailed to the resident within 30 days of termination or departure from the premises, whichever is later. Failure to provide this accounting and refund will bar the landlord from any claim for damages and require a full refund of the deposit. Bad faith on the part of the landlord could end in a civil penalty.

6.D.11   Where does the landlord go to evict a tenant?

Landlords apply to magistrate court for evictions.

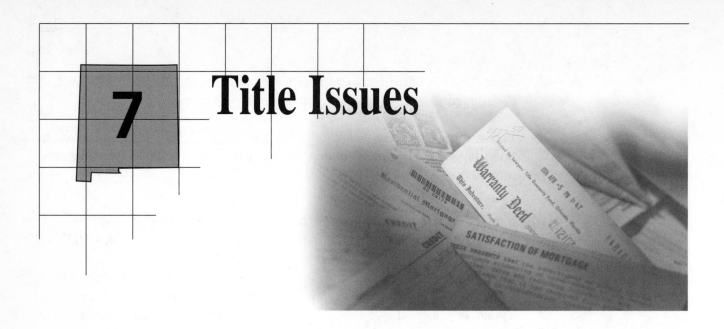

7 Title Issues

Encumbrances can affect the property's value, its title marketability, and its transferability. This chapter covers basic information about New Mexico-specific rules regarding property taxes; encumbrances such as licenses, easements, and adverse possession; and zoning regulations.

A. New Mexico Property Taxes

7.A.1 What is New Mexico's property tax year?

New Mexico's property tax year begins on January 1 of one calendar year and ends on December 31.

7.A.2 How are properties assessed?

Property is to be assessed at its fair market as of January 1 of the current tax year. Property valuation increases are capped at three percent over the previous year's value, or 6.1 percent over the previous two years' value. These "caps" would not apply in the case of new improvements to the property or in the year of transfer.

For example, the home is assessed for tax purposes at $100,000 for the current year. Twelve months later, the values in the area have gone up about 10 percent, but the new assessment can rise by only $3,000 (three percent of the previous year's value) to $103,000. Or the assessment after two years may be increased to $106,100. The reason for these caps is to permit reassessment on a regular basis but limit "sudden and huge" increases to the property owner.

7.A.3   Why do real estate licensees need to know about property tax computations?

Licensees should acquire basic knowledge about property tax assessments and time frames because property taxes can influence asking prices and offered prices. It is common for taxes to change when a property has been transferred to new owners. Licensees must also be aware that the buyer and seller are responsible for the reporting of the sale price within 30 days of transfer, most of the time this requirement is satisfied by title company personnel on behalf of buyers and sellers.

7.A.4   Can a property owner challenge a reassessment?

Yes. The property owner may challenge a reassessment by filing a protest with the Valuation Protest Board within 30 days of receiving the Notice of Valuation. At that time, the taxpayer can present evidence at the protest hearing to challenge the assessment amount. A property owner can also pay the disputed tax amount and seek a refund in District Court.

7.A.5   How are tax rates determined?

Tax rates are reflective of all approved state, county, city, school, and special budgets. Tax rates also consider all sources of income. After deducting the anticipated ancillary revenue derived from government reimbursements, gasoline taxes, fines, sales taxes, motel/hotel taxes, and so forth, from the approved budgets, the remainder necessary to cover the costs of the approved budgets is divided by the appropriate taxable value to determine the tax rate.

The tax ratio in New Mexico is 33 1/3 percent, so each property is taxed at one third of its assessed value.

Tax rates are quoted as dollars per thousand of net taxable value.

7.A.6   Is there any possibility of reductions in taxes due?

Yes, New Mexico allows for two exemptions. The head-of-household deduction is $2,000, and an eligible qualified veteran's exception is $3,000. Legislation also allows for a complete exemption from property tax for disabled veterans who build homes with federal grant funds. A "freeze" of assessed value is available for "lower-income" homeowners over age 65, and substantial reductions are available for agricultural property.

7.A.7   What is New Mexico's homestead exemption?

In New Mexico, some of the homestead of every person is exempt from judicial sale where there is no statutory declaration to the contrary. The homestead exemption is $30,000. Homestead protects the homeowner from a forced sale by any unsecured lienholder. Secured lienholders such as lenders and owners who sell on contract require that purchasers waive their homestead rights as a prerequisite to the contract.

7.A.8   When are property taxes due?

Taxes become a lien on January 1 of the year for which the taxes are due. The Notice of Valuation is mailed on April 1, and the owner has 30 days to challenge the assessment. Tax bills are mailed by October 10. Taxes are due and payable in two parts: November 10 of the current year and April 10 of the following year.

7.A.9   How are the due taxes paid when the property is sold?

When the property owner sells, taxes are divided into **current taxes** (those due but not delinquent) and **prorated taxes** (those due but not payable). Normally, the selling taxpayer pays the taxes that are due but not delinquent and prorates to the buyer those that are due but not payable. In some situations, these taxes owed by the seller can be quite substantial.

7.A.10   At what time must the taxes be paid to avoid penalties? What is the penalty?

In New Mexico, property taxes paid in installments require that the first installment be paid on or before November 10. The taxes are considered late on November 11. The second half installment is due before April 10 of the following year. There is no penalty for the first 30 days after the due dates. However, after that, the delinquent taxpayer is penalized one percent per month penalty (maximum of five percent) plus one percent interest per month. If taxes are delinquent after three years, the property may be sold at a tax sale.

7.A.11   At what point are properties ordered sold at a tax sale?

In New Mexico, property owners are allowed three years from the date of delinquency to make restitution and pay the appropriate penalty before the delinquent property is placed up for tax sale.

7.A.12   Does the delinquent taxpayer have any opportunity to "redeem" his or her property?

After a property is sold at a tax sale, the delinquent taxpayer has no right of redemption. An interested or secured party has up to two years to challenge the sale based on improper procedures. If all procedures were properly followed, there is no legal right to redeem. Should the sale be rescinded, the person who paid the taxes (who bought at the tax sale) is entitled to a return on his or her investment.

B.   Encumbrances

7.B.1   What are mechanics' liens?

A mechanic's lien is a statutory, equitable lien created in favor of contractors, laborers, and materialmen who have performed work or furnished materials in the erection or repair of a building and who have not been paid. The lien must be filed on the parcel of real estate where the material was used or the labor performed and must be filed in the county in which the real estate is located.

7.B.2   When do mechanics' liens apply? Who may claim them?

Suppliers of labor and materials under contract to improve a property may file a mechanic's lien if they have not been paid. Only licensed contractors may file a lien.

In New Mexico, mechanics' liens have priority over each other based on the delivery of materials or start of work (earliest). Original contractors must file the lien within 120 days of completion of work to keep the lien alive. All other claimants must file within 90 days. The lien remains valid for two years after filing.

It is possible for a mechanic's lien to be filed after closing, if the work had been performed within this time frame. It is effective as to the time that the work was performed. It might be noted that no notice must be given to the owner before filing a mechanic's lien.

7.B.3   What is a license?

The word *license* has different meanings. In real estate usage, it can mean permission. For example, someone can allow another to go hunting or fishing on his or her property or to enter the property to pick apples or get water from a spring. A **license** is personal privilege and, as such, it is considered to be *revocable permission,* not a right that transfers with ownership.

7.B.4   How may easements be created in New Mexico?

Easements in New Mexico can be created by deed or by use. Easements can be created by mutual agreement, and maintenance easements can be used in homeowner association agreements. If by deed, a licensed attorney should complete the deed.

A property owner may acquire a prescriptive easement by using someone else's property openly (visibly), notoriously, and without permission for a period of ten years. Tacking is used to determine the time frame that has passed, and a single owner is not required to have used the easement for the entire ten-year period.

7.B.5   What time frame must be observed for adverse possession (leading to ownership)?

To claim title to any ownership in real estate by adverse possession, a person must show that he or she has used the way, privilege, or other use openly, notoriously, and without permission for a period of at least ten years. Tacking is permitted. To prevent adverse possession, the owner must serve written notice to anyone using in the land in question that the owner intends to dispute any right arising from such claim or use.

7.B.6   Are there any other issues regarding encumbrances of which the licensee should be aware?

New Mexico utilizes statutory deed forms and statutory mortgage forms (meaning the forms are a part of state law, available through *www.conway-greene.com*). The period of statutory redemption after a judicial foreclosure sale is nine months. This can be waived by mutual agreement to not less than one month. Deeds of trust with the power of sale can be utilized only by mutual consent of the parties on transactions over $500,000, and the period before sale must be at least 180 days.

C. Zoning Issues

7.C.1   What is the source of zoning authority enjoyed by New Mexico communities?

The state of New Mexico gives the local municipalities and each local jurisdiction the right to develop their own zoning regulations. The regulations must promote the health, safety, morals, or the general welfare of the community. For all of the same reasons, the local jurisdictions are given the authority to regulate and restrict development.

7.C.2   Under what conditions may a developer subdivide?

To ensure harmonious growth with community standards, land developers must conform to the municipality's subdivision and land-development regulations. The land must be surveyed and laid out so that the subdivision utilizes natural drainage and land contours. Often an environmental impact report is required with the application for subdivision approval. Developers should be aware of the New Mexico Cultural Properties Act (see below and 4.F.5).

Plats have to be adopted by the municipality before they can be recorded. From the subdivision plans, plats are drawn of the land. The plat divides the land into lots. The plat is then submitted to the municipality for adoption. Often, the developer pays the costs for the streets and sewers, and the streets and sewers are then *dedicated* back to the municipality for its ownership and their future maintenance.

7.C.3   Are there any other issues of which to be aware?

Yes; the Cultural Properties Act provided for the creation of the Cultural Properties Review Committee (CPRC) to serve as a professional policy-making and advisory board for historic preservation in New Mexico. The act intends to promote activities to preserve the historic and prehistoric sites of New Mexico.

The CPRC works with property owners and administers state and federal rehabilitation tax credit programs to assist in preserving sites and to see that they are considered in planning for development. It maintains records, provides information and technical assistance, develops educational outreach programs, assists local governments in developing preservation ordinances and plans, and administers state and federal laws to help protect these properties.